Golf is a Funny Game
...But it Wasn't Meant to Be

GOLF
IS A FUNNY GAME
...but it wasn't meant to be

KEN JANKE

Momentum Books, Ltd.
Ann Arbor, Michigan

Illustrations and cover art © 1992 by Doug Parrish

Manufactured in the United States of America

1995   1994   1993   1992   5 4 3 2 1

Momentum Books Ltd.
210 Collingwood, Suite 106
Ann Arbor, Michigan 48103
U.S.A.

ISBN 1-879094-10-X

Library of Congress Cataloging-in-Publication Data

Janke, Ken, 1934–
    Golf is a funny game—but it wasn't meant to be : great golf quotes / Ken Janke : illustrations by Doug Parrish.
        p.   cm.
    Includes bibliographical references (p.   ).
    ISBN 1-879094-10-X (hardcover) : $21.95
    1. Golf—Quotations, maxims, etc.   I. Title.
GV965.J36   1992
796.352—dc20   92-4329
                                                         CIP

To...

Sally, who—despite her husband's addiction to golf—has managed to be understanding, supportive and loving;

...Our children, Ken, Laura and Julie, who never complained when their father stayed too long at the golf club;

...And the hundreds of golfers I have played with through the years and the many more I hope to play with in the future.

CONTENTS

FROM THE PUBLISHER

There are players of the game. There are students of it. Golf has legions of well-informed, articulate chroniclers and commentators. Then, there are those rare individuals whose knowledge of the game is so encompassing, whose love affair with it is so passionate, whose commitment to it is so consuming, that they can truly be called connoisseurs of the game of golf.

Within all these ranks, Ken Janke belongs. Comfortably, prominently.

His experiences on the golf course run the gamut from caddie to fine amateur player. His tales would fill another book. No set of volumes could contain his knowledge of the game. His personal golf library is astounding—more than 1,400 volumes. His contributions to golf literature are significant, for he fusses as much over the veracity of a detail about an article describing a long-ago event at his club, Indianwood, as he does a twisting down-hill five footer on its slippery greens.

That passion, that insight, that delight, he brings to these pages. Here, he offers the choicest comments on the choicest of games. Funny, perceptive and poignant. Distressed, bitter and anguished. Lyric, romantic and even rhapsodic. Quotes by caddies and celebrities. By kings, commoners and champions. The best of the best are here. The classic one-liners, the studied observations, the long-forgotten nuggets, the obscure and the never-before-in-print.

Each quote has been selected with care and insight by a man who has spent much of his life playing, studying, and adding to the richness and tradition of golf. This is Ken Janke's tribute to his game—that game of unlimited frustration, infinite variety, and finally supreme satisfaction.

But golf is also rich in the images of its players, caddies and settings. To capture such emotions and experiences in a single drawing takes not only a formidable talent but also a deep knowledge of the game. The illustrations of Doug Parrish that grace these pages give the most compelling evidence that he remains as comfortable with his pen as he was with a mashie in his fine playing days.

Ken Janke and Doug Parrish—a twosome paired up to provide thoughts and images about their favorite game. For your enjoyment. For posterity and golf.

Bill Haney
April 1992

FOREWORD

When it comes to golf, Ken Janke and I share a common heritage.

Every golfer remembers his or her introduction to the greats of the game, to those god-like people who hit the ball so well and so consistently it was hard to believe they were human. For me it was in 1945 when I saw an exhibition match between Byron Nelson and Jug McSpaden—the "gold-dust twins" as they were dubbed. That sparked my interest and when my father bought me a second-hand "set" of five Bobby Jones yellow-shafted Spaulding irons, I was hooked for life.

Most of the all-time greats are quoted or quoted about in these pages, including some who were special to me, such as fellow San Diegans Billy Casper and Gene Littler.

Virtually every sport has an oral tradition that has been captured on the printed page, but in terms of how much ink is expended in describing it, golf must be the champ. The game combines diverse elements in a majesty and with a drama and a humor that is unique. The variety of conditions under which golf is played, and the changes from one course to the next, stimulate a whole range of discussion unknown to other sports.

Just as the game itself demands creativity in conceiving a shot, so does it trigger the imagination to find the right phrase to describe it. As Ken Janke demonstrates in these pages, the equipment and the courses may have changed over the centuries, but one thing has not—the compulsion of golfers to find the most colorful ways to express their feelings about the game.

Golfers come in all shapes and sizes, but our language is a common and colorful one. An eighty-year-old golfing grandmother in Florida speaks the same language as do twenty-year-olds teeing it up in Tokyo, Mexico City or Madrid.

Reading Ken's book for the first time, I was struck with how similar golfers are across the oceans and over the centuries. A comment uttered in dismay after a mismanaged chip shot during a round in Scotland a hundred years ago would serve us splendidly today.

Ken has not rushed into writing this book. It's like sizing up a tricky putt: if you make it, the time was well spent. He started sizing up this book back in the '40's when he was caddying for the likes of Gene Sarazen and Jimmy Demaret. Since that time he had collected, sifted and compiled the choicest of the choice. Then, as sometimes happens in golf, Ken drew a great pairing. The outstanding artist Doug Parrish has captured the essence of the swings, the manner and the character of the all-time greats of the game to compliment Ken's text.

The result is as satisfying as a well-played round with just the right foursome on a sunny day when every drive finds the fairway and every putt finds the hole. Every time we open Ken Janke's book, we are transported to the greatest courses, the most thrilling matches, the magnetic moments of the most memorable characters in all the rich and timeless history of the greatest of all games.

Mickey Wright
April 1992

PREFACE

Most young boys who participate in sports have some heroes and I was no different. Initially they were Hank Greenberg of the Detroit Tigers and Joe Louis, the Heavyweight Champion of the World. Yes, I grew up in Detroit. A little later my father began to tell me about Ty Cobb, the "Georgia Peach," and about watching him at Navin Field. Here was a man with the highest lifetime batting average in baseball, not to mention the most stolen bases and hits for many decades. No one could tell me that Babe Ruth was better than Cobb, even with all of his home runs.

It was probably natural that I would end up with a golfing hero, too, after I became a caddie. The first was Jimmy Demaret, the dapper dresser who was the professional at Plum Hollow when I first began to tote bags there. Then Jimmy left and he was replaced by Sam Byrd, another big name in golf during the '40s. I wasn't the only caddie to wear a white visor, just like Byrd's. How I wish I still had that sweat-soaked thing with the signatures of Hogan, Nelson, Byrd and Mangrum on it.

We were lucky as caddies at Plum Hollow, not only because we had Mondays to play the course and act like the members, but because the club hosted tournaments and exhibitions. One of the events led to my first golf book purchase, part of a library which now includes more than 1,300 titles. In 1945, Plum Hollow sponsored the Big Fore Tournament. Of all the big names who participated fairly regularly on the tour at that time, only Sam Snead couldn't make it. He couldn't get leave from the Navy. He was replaced by Craig Wood, the U. S. Open champion of 1941 and, thus, the reigning champion. That wasn't too bad a name for a replacement. The others were Sam Byrd, Jug McSpaden and Byron Nelson.

Nelson was in the midst of a winning streak which would go down in history as one of the most amazing in golf. He would win 18 tournaments that year, 11 of them in a row. When an account of that year is reported now, even by the PGA, there is always a footnote that Nelson actually won a 12th during the streak, but it was not considered an official event since the prize money didn't meet the organization's minimum. Seldom mentioned is the fact that Nelson also lost one during that span. Perhaps it is dismissed because it was considered an exhibition rather than a tournament and the field was limited to four golfers, plus four Detroit All Stars who only participated for 36 holes. However, the event was 72 holes and had every aspect of a tournament, at least in my estimation.

When the Big Fore began, Lord Byron had won the last seven tournaments in which he played—the Miami Four-ball, Charlotte Open, Greensboro Open, Durham Open, Atlanta Open, Montreal Open and the Philadelphia Inquirer Invitational. Byrd opened with a 71 and was two behind Nelson, but took the lead after the second round when he shot a course record 64. Sam followed that up with 67 and another 64 to win going away. The amazing thing to me was that Byrd hit 71 of the 72 holes in regulation.

While I was happy that Byrd had won, I was impressed with Nelson and his friendly manner. In addition, there was no denying what a wonderful golfer he was and that his record was truly outstanding. In 1946, I learned that he was going to be at Hudson's, Detroit's largest department store, to sign copies of his book, *Winning Golf*. I was determined to buy a copy and arranged my day so that I would caddie one round in the morning and get downtown some way. Between hitchhiking and buses, I made it to Hudson's, paid my $3.50 and waited in line for Nelson to sign the book. Since a caddie's pay in those days was $1.50 for 18 holes, that was a big purchase and it was quite some time before I added the second book to my collection.

When I finished reading it, I wanted to find out more about golf and, fortunately, my father had some old copies of *The American Golfer* around the house. Much to my surprise, I found that golf had been played before Demaret, Nelson and Byrd. There had been players named Jones, Hagen, Sarazen and Armour who had won a lot of tournaments. The thing that caught my eye as I looked at the results of some of those events was that Walter Hagen was listed as playing out of Detroit. The more I read about him, the more I realized he was really a great golfer—

and he was from Detroit. Oh, I knew he was born in Rochester, but so what. Ty Cobb came from Georgia and Joe Louis was born in Alabama, so Walter Hagen could be my hero, too.

I will always remember playing in a junior golf tournament in 1950 sponsored by the YMCA. It was one of those days when things seemed to go right and my 74 was good enough for first place. I was invited back to the course a month later to collect my trophy and before it was presented to me, the chairman read a letter from Lyall Smith, sports editor of the *Detroit Free Press*. In it, he wrote that my 74 reminded him of a future Walter Hagen. How proud I was of that letter and I asked the chairman if I could have it. I cherished it more than the trophy and I still have it, yellow with age, in a treasured spot, safe in my home.

In 1949, Gene Sarazen was a frequent guest at Plum Hollow. He was employed by Joe Osplack, a member, who arranged for The Squire to play golf with customers. I was very excited the first time I was chosen to caddie for Sarazen. There was still a lot of good golf played by this man who first arrived on the scene in 1922 by winning the U. S. Open. As the weeks passed, I caddied regularly for Sarazen. It was still special for me, but not as much as the first time.

I realized that even the great professionals hit errant shots now and then. One of them I will never forget. On the 11th hole, his tee shot sliced down a hill where plum trees once grew, giving the name to the golf club. It was extremely wet and balls would bury so the only way to find them was from the angle they entered the bog. We all searched for his ball, but to no avail. Sarazen was not in the best of humor, having just made a bogey on the previous hole. I naturally got the blame for not finding the ball, which was perfectly logical. After all, part of a caddie's job is to know where the ball is and I failed to do that in this instance. Still, I felt I was getting a little too much heat since most balls hit into that area were lost.

In this case, Sarazen seemed to be taking his frustration out on me and I retaliated saying, "Here you are one of the greatest golfers in the world and you're blaming me because you hit a big slice." He looked at me and began to laugh, put his arm around me and said, "You're right. Let's go back and hit another one." When the hole was completed, I stood at the 12th tee with the other caddies and Mr. Osplack approached me. Very sternly he said, "If you ever talk to Mr. Sarazen like that again, I'll make sure you get fired." All I could reply was, "Yes, sir."

Sarazen told a lot of stories during those rounds, mostly entertaining the customers. Naturally, I listened. Many centered around Hagen and Jones. I could tell that Sarazen greatly admired both, but at the same time felt he was their equal. If there was one golfer whom Sarazen really admired, it was Harry Vardon. One story which he told over and over was about Vardon's accuracy. He said that Vardon was so accurate, he couldn't play two rounds on the same course on the same day because in the second round he would hit his drives into the divots he had made in the morning. That story, of course, has been repeated by countless people many times. It wasn't until recently, however, that I read a comment by Charles Price that showed how silly that story was. In the article he wondered if Vardon was really that accurate, why didn't he miss the divots on purpose?

Many of Sarazen's stories centered around his exhibitions with Hagen as well as competing against the Haig. There was just no question in my mind that Hagen was bigger than life and how I wished I could see him in person some day.

The stories I heard about Hagen seemed too good to be true. Later I discovered many had been somewhat embellished by the teller. Still, the stories were enough to make him a special person to me. One of the first quotes I recall hearing from a golfer came from Hagen, even though it didn't really deal with golf. It was, "Never hurry and don't worry. You're here just for a short visit. So don't forget to stop and smell the flowers along the way." What a wonderful philosophy on life.

When I read his book, which was published in 1956, I penciled his quote on a piece of paper and later began to jot down other quotes about golf that had a special meaning to me. Then, I began to put them into a notebook by subject. From that point, I actually searched out quotes with the thought of someday putting them all into a book.

While the quotes come from many different sources, there were three writers who contributed more than others, and whose thoughts and reflections I felt were the most meaningful. First was Bernard Darwin, the grandson of the famous naturalist who had the ability to put words together in a way since unmatched. He was certainly an authority on the game, having seen the greats from John Ball, Harry Vardon, James Braid and J. H. Taylor to Bobby Jones, Walter Hagen and Gene Sarazen.

The second is, in my opinion, the best of the American golf writers, Herbert Warren Wind. He helped me to appreciate Darwin. Perhaps because I thought it would flatter Wind, I told him that I wasn't impressed with Bernard Darwin and his opinions. It was probably based on my feeling that Darwin showed a bias toward British golfers to the detriment of the Americans. That was only normal, Wind said, adding he felt Darwin was quite fair to the Americans, while still showing national pride.

Wind wrote for *The New Yorker* for many years and I always looked forward to his articles about the Masters and U. S. Open. He gave the reader the feeling that he was actually at the tournament. When he described a golf course, you could see the bunkers and contour of the green. His books are classics and a must for any golf library.

My other favorite golf writer is Charles Price. He is the only writer I know who could write an entire column on the proper use of the word "bunker" or the difference between a foursome and a four-ball, keeping the reader glued to the page. He was a fair golfer in his younger years, so there was an authority to his writing. He never backed off from offering an opinion, whether about an over-rated golf course or a pretender to the crown worn by Jack Nicklaus.

If there are more quotes about certain golfers or courses, it is because more has been written about them. Fifty years from now, we may find more mention of Tom Watson's ability than we do today. Time is needed to fully appreciate a golfer's record and accomplishments, just as time is needed for a golf course to mature.

It is my hope that other golfers will enjoy reading the quotes as much as I have enjoyed collecting them.

K.J.
April 1992

ACKNOWLEDGEMENTS

A great many people have contributed to this book and the most obvious are the golf writers and golfers who are quoted throughout. But indirectly there are even more. They are the people who made golf so enjoyable for me. Without that love of the game there would be no book.

It began with my father, who took me to the course when I was a five-year-old, not so much to teach me golf initially, but so my mother could get a break from watching over a very active young boy. I was told where to stand and above all, to be quiet. It didn't stop me from grabbing a club and trying to imitate their swings when the golfers had put their bags on the ground while they were putting.

Eventually my dad saw I wanted to play and we made a visit to a pawn shop where he purchased a "set" of seven clubs for me, no two of which were made by the same manufacturer. He paid a princely sum of $3, still I thought it was the most magnificent set ever produced. He painfully measured each club, removed the grips, sawed off the hickory shafts to the right length and then replaced the slippery, leather grips which covered most of the shaft.

Now the trips to the course took on a new meaning. He stuffed my clubs into his bag along with his seven. I was allowed to play those holes which were out of sight of the starter. (My father was not one to throw money around and the 25 cents greens fee in 1939 was a sizeable outlay.) Without question, it was my dad who got me started, but there were many more along the way:

My family, Sally, Ken, Laura and Julie, for their complete devotion and understanding;

The members of Plum Hollow where I really learned to play the game; the first and last caddiemasters I had, Bill Uzelac and Bill Langnau, who treated me as if I was a member of their family;

My partners through the years who helped me win and didn't blame me when we lost, which happened more frequently: Lee Anderson, Lem

Barney, George Bayer, Ron Bernas, Faust Bianco, Gene Bone, Henry Britt, Murray Brooks, Bob Burger, John Butash, Bill Curtis, Larry Dailey, Al Dittrich, Don Dulude, Jerry Dziedzic, Randy Erskine, Joe Fair, Jim Feehley, William Clay Ford, Ed Furgol, John Ginopolis, Pete Green, Walter Hagen, Jr., Mike Helmer, Dave Hill, Dick Holthaus, Linc Jackson, Lynn Janson, Ben Jaroslaw, Cass Jawor, John Jawor, Glenn Johnson, Walter Kirchberger, Kenny Knox, Chuck Kocsis, Lou Koller, Ron Kondratko, Ron Kramer, John Lathan, Orv Lefko, Rayme Martin, Bill Mattson, Bob McMasters, Al Mengert, Joe Michael, Charlie Moore, Ron Nichols, Ed Nicholson, Minoro Nakai, Pete Olar, Yoshiki Otaki, Dave Parker, Penny Pennington, George Plimpton, Bob Pryor, Bob Rivest, Lew Rockwell, Glenn Rosso, Bill Rogers, Jeff Roth, Greg Ruddy, Jack Saylor, Bob Schleh, Joe Schmidt, Don Sherer, Wiffi Smith, Jerry Stawora, Bud Stevens, Don Stevens, Jack Stocker, Larry Tomasino, Evan "Big Cat" Williams, Al Wygant and Dave Zink;

Doug Parrish, an outstanding illustrator whose unique drawings reflect his love of the game;

The members of Indianwood and Stan Aldridge who transformed the club into one of the finest in the country. They really deserve the high ranking bestowed on the course by *Golf Magazine;*

Members of the Golf Collectors' Society, especially Joe Murdoch for his encouragement and direction;

Don Danko, the editor of *Better Investing,* for reading the copy and making numerous suggestions as did Bill Haney, the publisher;

And, finally, the golf professionals who were my heros in days past, Sam Byrd, Jimmy Demaret, Walter Hagen, Ben Hogan, Ky Laffoon, Lloyd Mangrum, Byron Nelson, Gene Sarazen, Al Watrous and the greatest woman golfer of all-time, Mickey Wright.

K.J.

1

The Game

Golf has been called the sport of princes on down to some unprintable names. Call it what you wish, once you take up the game, it's usually for life. The more you study golf, the more complicated it seems to become and the puzzle is why it is so difficult.

I can remember hearing a story during my caddie days of Sam Snead hitting some golf balls at Briggs Stadium before a baseball game. As the story was related to me, the Tigers were playing the Red Sox, so Ted Williams was in town. After Snead had finished hitting the shots into the bleachers with some short iron, Williams supposedly told him that Snead was lucky to be playing such an easy game. After all, the ball just sat there and Snead only had to hit it. In baseball the ball was moving, sometimes at incredible speeds or curving. Now, that was a difficult sport. Snead's response was something to the effect that while that may be true, Williams never had to go and hit his foul balls.

That story has probably been told in a number of ways with the cast of characters and the location changed depending on who told the story and where. Still, it touches on one of the differences between golf and other sports. Of course, there are many.

Every pitcher's rubber is exactly 60 feet, 6 inches from home plate. Every football field is 100 yards long, plus the end zones. In short, there is an exactness to dimensions in most sports, except golf. The governing bodies of golf, the USGA and the R&A, have certain specifications for the size of a golf ball and the grooves on a club, but only guidelines as to a hole. The design of the hole is an individual thing. The opening hole at the Old Course is not the same as the one at Pebble Beach. Not all par-fours are 400 yards long. Some are shorter and may even be more difficult than their longer counter-parts. In fact, the same hole can be different day to day because of the pin position, weather or wind direction.

The field of play is not the only thing which sets golf apart. It is, however, a big part of the difference and has evoked countless hours of discussion. Possibly the only thing courses have in common, at least those which are tournament sites, is that they all seem to have a great finishing hole.

A basketball player pretends he is fouled so he can go to the free throw line. A baseball player claims he caught the ball, even when he traps it and so does a receiver in football. Would you ever expect a catcher to turn to the umpire and tell him the pitch was actually outside after the umpire had called a strike? In so many sports there is the tendency to deceive and there are officials ready to call an immediate infraction. Not so in golf. The game is built on honesty. If the ball moves, the player calls a penalty on himself. Sure, there are some who cheat, but mostly it is a game of honor and there are far more honest players than others.

A golfer need not have an opponent to enjoy the game. He can play against the course and try to improve his skills without participating in a tournament. To score better than ever before is enough of an accomplishment. It doesn't have to be a course record.

The average baseball player doesn't have the opportunity to stand at home plate and see if he can hit the ball into the stands like Hank Aaron. But the average golfer can stand on the first tee and compare his drive with the one Jack Nicklaus hit on the same hole in a tournament just weeks before. If a weekend tennis player goes up against Boris Becker, there is no handicap devised which will let him have a chance against such a player. In golf, the handicap system, while still favoring the more accomplished golfer, offers an opportunity for some real competition between the scratch player and the one who plays to a 20 handicap. Nor is age a problem in golf as it is in other sports. The ball need not be hit a long distance just to compete. A senior can hold his own against someone half his age. In 1990, a friend, Bob McMasters, won both the club championship and the senior championship at his golf club. That's akin to Jack Kramer winning a 50-and-over tournament and winning at Wimbledon the same year. It just doesn't happen very often.

Perhaps the biggest difference between golf and other games is that a golfer has time to think about what he is going to do next. Some say that is an advantage, but actually it works against and not for the golfer. When motor skills are learned, they can be repeated in reaction sports. That's not always the case in golf. How else can you explain what happens to a golfer who shanks a simple nine-iron to the last green after he has hit every approach to the pin in the previous 71 holes? That can happen to the finest professional on tour. Why does someone miss a straight two-foot putt, uphill, when he has practiced on the green for two hours every day over the past 10 years? It's in the mind. You must think, not just react.

Golfers have been known to play 18 holes in one day, each hole on a different course. They have played on three continents in the same day. When rubber was not available during World War II, balls were fashioned out of wood. In Africa, one course allows a free drop from elephant footprints. At an Arizona course, one local rule calls for a free drop of two club lengths from a rattlesnake.

Golf has caused divorces. Wedding vows have included golfing rights. Some have lost jobs because of the game. Charles Blair Macdonald, the first U.S. Amateur champion, cut his son-in-law out of his will as a result of an off-hand remark about the first hole at the National Golf Links which Macdonald had designed. No wonder so much has been written about the game.

There is no game like golf. It can be an obsession for some while others refuse to ever pick up another club. There is, perhaps, no adequate way to explain golf although many have tried. One thing is certain. There is no gray area. You either love it or you hate it.

"The Londoner who declares golf a moral game is all wrong. Golf is anything but a moral pastime. It is essentially and in all its phases immoral. Golf is followed by a set of Cyrenaic sensuists as corrupt in their philosophy and profane in their doctrines as ever Aristippus was. They are a set of hedonistic Hottentots who find in golf the consummate answer to the proposition that the greatest good is the gratification of the senses."

St. Louis Republic editorial
in 1905

"Golf has so many virtues; it is not too strenuous; it is healthy; it can be played, anyhow in our climate, practically the whole year round. It has so many advantages over all other games that it must endure and prosper."

Lord Brabazon of Tara,
1952

"It is a thousand pities that neither Aristotle nor Shakespeare was a golfer. There is no other game that strips the soul so naked."

Horace Hutchinson

"Unlike many sports, golf does not enjoy the privilege of knowing its exact birthright."

Ian Morrison, 1990

"Because golf exposes the flaws of the human swing—a basically simple maneuver—it causes more self-torture than any game short of Russian roulette."

Grantland Rice, 1954

"Its fascinations have always been gratefully acknowledged, and not a few of its worthier practioners have from time to time in prose and verse, rehearsed its praises."

Robert Clark, 1875

"No one remembers who was second."

Walter Hagen

"Gof is an exercise which is much used by the Gentlemen of Scotland. A large common in which there are several little holes is chosen for the purpose. It is played with little leather balls stuffed with feathers; and sticks made somewhat in the form of a handy-wicket. He who puts a ball into a given number of holes, with the fewest strokes, gets the game."

Benjamin Rush, 1771. Rush was one of the signers of the Declaration of Independence

"When you fall in love with golf, you seldom fall easy. It's obsession at first sight."

Thomas Boswell, 1990

"If profanity had an influence on the flight of the ball, the game would be played far better than it is."

Horace Hutchinson, 1886

"Golf is deceptively simple, endlessly complicated. A child can play it well, and a grown man can never master it. Any single round of it is full of unexpected triumphs and seemingly perfect shots that end in disaster. It is almost a science, yet it is a puzzle without an answer. It is gratifying and tantalizing, precise and unpredictable. It requires complete concentration and total relaxation. It satisfies the soul and frustrates the intellect. It is at the same time rewarding and maddening—and it is without doubt the greatest game mankind has ever invented."

Robert Forgan

"It is not a matter of life and death. It is not that important. But it is a reflection of life, and so the game is an enigma wrapped in a mystery impaled on a conundrum."

Peter Alliss, 1989

"No athletic game affords such opportunity for cool calculation or such occasion for self-examination and self-castigation as golf."

John L. Low, 1903

"A great deal of unnecessarily bad golf is played in this world."

Harry Vardon, 1922

"Of this diversion the Scots are so fond, that, when the weather will permit, you may see a multitude of all ranks, from the senator of justice to the lowest tradesman, mingled together, in their shirts, and following the balls with utmost eagerness."

Thomas Smollett, 1771

"A tolerable day, a tolerable green, a tolerable opponent, supply, or ought to supply, all that any reasonably constituted human being should require in the way of entertainment."

A. J. Balfour, 1890

"Remember that it is always possible to 'overgolf' yourself. Two rounds a day is enough for any man with a week or more of solid golf in front of him."

Horace Hutchinson, 1896

"Yes, it is a cruel game, one in which the primitive instincts of man are given full play, and the difference between golf and fisticuffs is that in one the pain is of the mind and in the other it is of the body."

Henry Leach, 1914

"The game lends itself to fantasies about our abilities."

Peter Alliss, 1981

"Royal and Ancient the game may well be named, for at least six ruling monarchs of the Stuart line were golfers."

Robert H. K. Browning, 1955

"Playing golf is like learning a foreign language."

Henry Longhurst, 1937

"Any game where a man 60 can beat a man 30 ain't a game."

Burt Shotten, former manager of the Brooklyn Dodgers

"Golf obviously provides one of our best forms of healthful exercise accompanied by good fellowship and companionship."

Dwight D. Eisenhower,
1953

"He who has fastest golf cart never have bad lie."

Mickey Mantle, 1962

"If a man can shoot 10 birdies, there's no reason why he can't shoot 18. Why can't you birdie every hole on the course?"

Ben Hogan, 1941

"Moderation is essential in all things, madam, but never in my life have I been beaten by a teetotaler."

Harry Vardon, to a woman wanting him to sign the pledge

"The problem with golf is I have to deal with a humiliation factor."

George H. W. Bush

"Golf is a game of the head as well as a game of the hands."

Jerome Travers, 1913

"I never played a round when I didn't learn something new about the game."

Ben Hogan

"From its earliest beginning, golf has been a gentleman's game—to be played as much for the sake of the game as for the contest."

Tony Lema, 1966

"Golf charms by its infinite variety."

Theodore Moone

"There is no special age for learning to play golf, but it is better not to postpone the attempt till after 50."

Arnaud Massy, 1911

"I think golf is good for boxing, but the reverse is far from being the case."

Max Baer, former heavy-weight champion, 1939

"Golf is in the interest of good health and good manners. It promotes self-restraint and, as one of its devotees has well said, affords a chance to play the man and act the gentleman."

William Howard Taft

"Golf is a game in which attitude of mind counts for incomparably more than mightiness of muscle."

Arnold Haultain, 1908

"With any other sport or pastime golf compares favourably."

Sir W. G. Simpson

"Golf, after all, is probably the universal sport."

Lorne Rubenstein

"Golf is an 'umblin' game."

George Low

"In golf, as in no other sport, your principal opponent is yourself."

Herbert Warren Wind

"I never learned anything from a match that I won."

Robert T. Jones, Jr.

"It can be asserted with total confidence that one of the most important reasons why we golfers believe golf to be the finest of all games is that it is played in beautiful surroundings."

Peter Dobereiner, 1978

"Pressure is playing a five-dollar Nassau with only a dollar in your pocket."

Lee Trevino

"Golf keeps the heart young and the eyes clear."

Andra Kirkaldy, 1921

"It was one of Scotland's greatest gifts to modern civilization."

Charles Mortimer, 1952

"Golf is a game not just of manners but of morals."

Art Spander

"No man ever will have golf under his thumb. No round ever will be so good it could not have been better. Perhaps that is why golf is the greatest of games."

Robert T. Jones, Jr.

"That little white ball just sits there. A man can beat himself before he ever swings at it."

Ellsworth Vines, tennis great
turned professional golfer

"Whatever anyone may care to say about golf, at least one thing is mercifully certain, namely that it is a voluntary affair."

Henry Longhurst, 1955

"The steps you hit your drive past your opponent are the most golden you'll walk in your life."

Paul Berthody

"My love of golf is part of my religion. I introduce the game to friends and other people constantly, hoping they will get from it what I have."

Bill Blue, LPGA Commissioner, 1989

"Par is a designation of excellence."

Robert Sommers, 1974

"Golf is a game of emotion. If you can't control your emotions, you can't play golf."

Ben Hogan, 1976

"In golf you almost always beat yourself or are destroyed by the game."

Al Barkow, 1976

"Golf, for all the appearance of tame tranquility that it is apt to present to the uninitiated mind, provides a more searching test of nerve and temperament than any other game in the world."

Harry Vardon, 1922

"Golf is a peculiar game of a peculiar people."

John L. Low, 1903

"After all, as every golfer in every land will attest after a good round, it may well be the best game ever invented."

Herbert Warren Wind

"Tennis is like a wonderful, longstanding relationship with a husband. Golf is a tempestuous, lousy lover; it's totally unpredictable, a constant surprise."

Dinah Shore

"Golf is a compromise between what your ego wants you to do, what experience tells you to do, and what your nerves let you do."

Bruce Crampton

"Why do we work so hard to feel so terrible?"

Hollis Stacy

"I'd rather make the cut in the Crosby than win another Oscar."

Jack Lemmon

"Golf's a puzzle without an answer. It's the most exact sport I know of. It's unpredictable."

Gary Player

"In any other sport, it's considered semi-honorable, even chuckle-creating, to cheat."

Jim Murray

"I like trying to win. That's what golf is all about."

Jack Nicklaus

"Of all the games man has devised, supposedly for his enjoyment, golf is in a class by itself in the anguish it inflicts."

Herbert Warren Wind

"It ain't how in this game. It's how many."

Lloyd Mangrum

"By the time you get dressed, drive out there, play 18 holes and come home, you've blown seven hours. There are better things you can do with your time."

Richard M. Nixon

"I go to sleep when I watch golf on television."

George Archer, 1989

"I started out 8, 6, 8 and then I blew up."

Tony Mullas, 1950, on caddie
day at Plum Hollow

"Golf is deceptively simple and endlessly complicated."

Arnold Palmer

"Ninety percent of golf is played from the shoulders up."

Deacon Palmer

"Golf being a cold, calculating sort of game gives perhaps more scope for folly than any other. We have all the time in the world to make up our minds as to what is the wise thing to do and then we do the foolish one."

Bernard Darwin, 1937

"Cheap golf, it is accepted, is the Scotsman's birthright."

Peter Dobereiner, 1970

"There are three types of golf—golf, tournament golf and major championship golf."

Grantland Rice

"Golf comes third behind my family and my religion. If I had to give up one of the three, it would be golf."

Johnny Miller

"A game in which you can claim the privilege of age and retain the playthings of childhood."

Samuel Johnson

"The trouble with golf is you're only as good as your last putt."

Doug Sanders

"Golf is the Esperanto of sport. All over the world golfers talk the same language—much of it nonsense and much unprintable—endure the same frustrations, discover the same infallible secrets of putting, share the same illusory joys."

Henry Longhurst

"It can be played and enjoyed by children and elderly people, but it is neither 'child's play' nor an 'old man's game.' Golf has more than enough to it to command the respect of any man whatever his physical or mental stature."

Robert T. Jones, Jr.

"The game embarrasses you until you feel inadequate."

Ben Crenshaw

"When I first witnessed golf in Scotland it looked to me like a silly game for old men."

Charles Blair Macdonald, 1928

"Ever since golf began—Scottish historians have settled on the year 1100 as a reasonable date of birth—the game has been an enigma."

Herbert Warren Wind

"On the golf course a man may be the dogged victim of the inexorable fate, be struck down by an appalling stroke of tragedy, become the hero of a side-splitting comedy—any of those within a few hours, and all without having to bury a corpse or repair a tangled personality."

Robert T. Jones, Jr.

"Golf is the loneliest of all games, not excluding postal chess."

Peter Dobereiner, 1970

"It is a game of skill, needing mind and thought and judgment. As well as a cunning hand."

James Balfour

"That little ball won't move until you hit it, and there's nothing you can do for it after it has gone."

Mildred "Babe" Zaharias

"There is not the slightest doubt in my own mind that golf as played in the United States is the slowest in the world."

Henry Longhurst

"The pleasures of golf are increased a thousandfold when it is played correctly."

Alex Herd, 1923

"Few learn golf in a lifetime."

Grantland Rice

"Over the centuries golf has evolved from a pastime to a game, a competition, sometimes a profession and, for most of us, a passion that transcends mere play."

Robert Trent Jones, 1988

"Golf will grow so long as it's fun."

Tom Watson, 1978

"Golf is a wonderful game. It is the only one played on natural terrain or on grounds made to resemble gently rolling linksland. It is the one outdoor game in which a stationary player hits a stationary ball. The fact that a player must generate his own power is one of the fundamental reasons that golf is perhaps the most difficult of all the major games to play consistently well."

Herbert Warren Wind

"In almost every country in the world, golf is played on a 'grander' and more expensive scale than in Britain."

Henry Longhurst, 1963

"Golf to me is not a business; it's an art form, like a Picasso or a Steinbeck novel."

Tom Watson, 1978

"There is a constant confrontation with the elements. There is a great challenge to the physical skills and to the mind. It is at once an art and a test of strength. There is always the need to perform a stroke of uncommon precision, none ever really the same, each requiring absolute control of the muscles and the emotions, a mastery of self. Sometimes we accomplish this, but often we do not. So there is exhilaration . . . and there is frustration. There is triumph and tragedy. Usually there is all of this within a single round, often within a single hole."

Robert Trent Jones, 1988

"Nothing is predictable in the game of golf."

Jim Warters, 1980

"I don't know how I would ever have been able to look into the past with any degree of pleasure or enjoy the present with any degree of contentment if it had not been for the extraordinary influence the game of golf has had upon my welfare."

Charles Blair Macdonald, 1928

"Golf is like love. One day you think you are too old and the next day you want to do it again."

Roberto de Vicenzo, 1989

"Whatever resemblances there are between golf and other ancient games, the simple truth remains that it was the Scots who first combined in a game the characteristics of hitting a ball cross-country, to a hole in the ground without interference by an opponent."

Charles Price, 1962

"It is, nevertheless, a game of considerable passion, either of the explosive type, or that which burns inwardly and sears the soul."

Robert T. Jones, Jr., 1962

"Say what you like, long driving is THE fascination of golf. People will talk for hours on the theory of putting, on lateral hip shifts, forward presses, delayed wrist action and all the rest of it, but the thing which appeals to the heart of every golfer great and small is big hitting."

Henry Longhurst, 1957

"In golf you've got two continuously merciless competitors: yourself and the course."

Tommy Armour, 1959

"Splosh! One of the finest sights in the world: the other man's ball dropping in the water—preferably so that he can see it but cannot quite reach it and has therefore to leave it there, thus rendering himself so mad that he loses the next hole as well."

Henry Longhurst, 1959

"The more you learn about games, the more you are apt to realize the number of things golf doesn't have. It doesn't have the effervescent excitement with which football is blessed. It hasn't the grand strategy from which baseball largely derives its popular appeal. It does not require the stamina of tennis, the self-confidence of bowling, the finesse of billiards, the concentration of bridge, the intuition of chess. Yet, at its best, golf commands all these things—and much more—something which probably cannot be said about any other game."

Charles Price, 1962

"Golf has been called 'the most human of games' and a 'reflection of life.' One reason that we enjoy it and that it challenges us is that it enables us to run the entire gamut of human emotions, not only in a brief space of time, but likewise without measurable damage either to ourselves or to others."

Robert T. Jones, Jr., 1962

"Golf is the game of a lifetime."

Tony Lema, 1966

"It is the constant and undying hope for improvement that makes golf so exquisitely worth the playing."

Bernard Darwin

"Golf is like solitaire. When you cheat, you cheat only yourself."

Tony Lema, 1966

"Fashions come and go in golf clubs as they do in clothes and often what is hailed as the latest thing is only a revival of what was all the rage 50 years ago."

Henry Longhurst, 1962

"The game has its sensuous pleasures, when you make the perfect swing and execute the shot precisely as you had planned it."

Peter Alliss, 1981

"Every ball maker all over the world, according at any rate to the advertisements, makes a ball which goes farther than everybody else's."

Henry Longhurst, 1966

"Three things there are as unfathomable as they are fascinating to the masculine mind: metaphysics, golf and the feminine heart."

Arnold Haultain, 1908

"Golf may be a hussy, but I love her."

Don Herold, 1952

"Golf is not a mere game; it is a disease, infectious and contagious, which once acquired cannot be shaken off. Once a golfer, always a golfer—there's no help for it."

L. Latchford, 1903

"In the early 1880s golf was, if I may so term it, a much cosier game than it is now, because there were so many fewer people playing it that they all had something of a fraternal sentiment towards one another."

Bernard Darwin, 1931

"Golf is a game with a shady past. Its actual birth is shrouded in mystery. No one is quite certain when or where it drew its first tortured breath."

Will Grimsley, 1966

"Golf is more than a mere game. It is a religion."

Walter Travis

"Golf is a gentleman's game and a golfer should be courteous, polite and unselfish."

Jerome Travers, 1913

"Next to the idiotic, the dull unimaginative mind is the best for golf."

Sir Walter Simpson

"There is probably no game which affords a greater scope than golf for all possible forms of nervousness, not only for sheer terror but for every conceivable foolish fancy which can impair the properly concentrated frame of mind."

Bernard Darwin, 1912

"It does look like a very good exercise. But what is the little white ball for?"

Ulysses S. Grant, after watching a beginner swing several times without making contact with the ball

"At first blush golf may strike the unitiated as an easy game, but the moment they try it, they will realise that, in order to hit the ball properly and to impel it from hole to hole in the smallest possible number of strokes, it is necessary to study thoroughly the science and technique of this most complicated game."

Arnaud Massy, 1911

"I have often been gratefully aware of the heroic efforts of my opponents not to laugh at me."

Bernard Darwin, 1934

"The main object of the game of golf is to get the ball in the hole in the fewest possible number of strokes."

Walter Travis, 1901

"What I do not know is why so many people are content to play so badly. Some people play only three or four times a year, and you don't expect much from them, but others play every week and they can be quite dreadful."

Peter Alliss, 1981

"My golf is woeful but I will never surrender."

Bing Crosby

"Golf gives you an insight into human nature, your own as well as your opponent's. Eighteen holes of match or medal play will teach you more about your foe than will 18 years of dealing with him across a desk."

Grantland Rice, 1954

"Would that I could hand on unimpaired the great game as it was my good fortune to know it!"

Charles Blair Macdonald

"Golf is a game of situations."

John L. Low, 1903

"Golf can be one of the most grueling and frustrating activities devised by man, demanding total commitment. The mind, the body and the spirit must blend as one in an act of creation rather than reaction."

Lew Fishman, 1980

"The more you play it the less you know about it."

Patty Berg, 1937

"Golf literally may be said to be in Scotland a game of immemorial antiquity."

Robert Clark, 1875

"This game is so elusive. You try to maintain the peaks and level up the valleys."

Tom Watson, 1979

"Golf is very unpredictable."

Seve Ballesteros, 1990

"Golf is not sacred, and there's no use getting so gosh-darned solemn about it."

Don Herold, 1952

"Golf is, in part, a game; but only in part. It is also in part a religion, a fever, a vice, a mirage, a frenzy, a fear, an abscess, a joy, a thrill, a pest, a disease, an uplift, a brooding melancholy, a dream of yesterday, a disappointing today and a hope for tomorrow."

Grantland Rice, 1926

"Don Quixote would understand golf. It is the impossible dream."

Jim Murray, 1988

"Golf is at least a 50 percent mental game, and if you recognize that it is in the mind that prompts us physically then you can almost say that golf is entirely a mental game."

Peter Thomson, 1961

"Always remember that however good you may be the game is your master."

                                                    J. H. Taylor

"Golf is so popular because it is the best game in the world at which to be bad."

                                                    A. A. Milne, 1919

"Golf is a gentleman's game but from some of the remarks that are bandied about during a round and following a 'friendly' game, one often wonders how long a gentleman can remain a gentleman and still play golf."

                                                    Des Sullivan

"The game of golf is between your mind and your fingers. If you take your mind off your hands you're a dead pigeon."

                                                    Jerry Barber

"The basic problem with golf, aside from the fact it's nearly impossible to play, is that intrinsically it's a game between a man and nature, you against the world."

                                                    Art Spander

"The real success in golf lies in turning three shots into two,"

                                                    Bobby Locke

"For this game you need, above all things, to be in a tranquil frame of mind."

                                                    Harry Vardon, 1921

"In truth the game is one of the most exasperating hitherto devised by the wit of man."

H. S. C. Everard, 1896

"Golf at its best should be a contest of risks."

John L. Low, 1903

"I wish to emphasize that there are no secrets to golf."

Ernest Jones, 1953

"There is cruelty in golf, cold, hurting cruelty in this game. If now you hesitate, consider. The difference between the effect of boxing and the effect of golf on the human system is that golf hurts more and the pain is more enduring, for it is psychological."

Henry Leach, 1914

"Golf can be annoying but you like it."

Robert Cromie

"To some minds the great field which golf opens up for exaggeration is its chief attraction. Lying about the length of one's drives has this advantage over most forms of falsehood, that it can scarcely be detected."

Sir W. G. Simpson, 1892

"Even if that handicap is going up, to play golf worse than we used to do is better than to play none at all."

Bernard Darwin

"Long driving, if it be not the most deadly, is certainly the most dashing and fascinating part of the game; and of all others the principal difficulty of the Golfer to acquire, and his chief delight when he can manage it."

Henry Brougham Farnie,
1857

"When everything has been said, however, the fact remains that golf is a splendid game, and has, moreover, a charm impossible to describe or exaggerate."

R. H. Lyttleton, 1901

2

Players of the Game

There's no such thing as a typical golfer. They come in all sizes, shapes and ages. The range of ability is as diverse as that of a Mickey Mantle down to a beginning Little Leaguer. One of my favorite members as a caddie was Harry Armstrong. He couldn't play a lick, but he enjoyed golf so much, even the matches in the 10th flight. Once he made six on the final hole and it was like he had just won the Masters. It was the first time Mr. Armstrong had ever broken 100. I was rewarded with a $20 bill, an enormous amount considering the normal rate was $1.50.

Holes-in-one have been recorded by a six-year-old as well as Otto Bucher, who was 99 when he aced a 130-yard hole in 1985. Some play a lifetime and never have that thrill, while others hole a tee shot almost annually. James Simpson played golf for 81 years and finally made his first hole-in-one when he was 89 years old.

Jim Hart was 17 when he won his first club championship at Fox Hills Country Club. In 1990 he was 75 when he won it for the fifth time.

Some people consider themselves golfers even though they play only once or twice a year. At last count, J. J. Johnston of Fort Worth had played 2,039 consecutive days. That's more than five and a half years of continuous golf.

At times there is the impression that all of the tour players are six feet, blond and have flat bellies. But Ed Oliver tipped the scales at better than 250 pounds and was a successful tournament golfer. No one called him Ed. It was always Porky. Willie Wood, Lee Trevino and Jeff Sluman are all 5' 7" although Willie must have been measured while standing on a platform. Ian Woosnam is shorter than all three but longer off the tee than all of them. Fred McLeod weighed only 108 pounds when he captured the U.S. Open in 1908. George Bayer and George Archer are both 6' 5" and each won his share of tournaments.

In spite of the many differences, those who play golf still have much in common. They all hit some good shots and some terrible ones. When the pressure is on they choke, some more often than others. At other times, the 20 handicapper hits the shot of his life under pressure and might never duplicate the shot in 100 more attempts. Most of all, regardless of skill level, the golfer strives to improve—and this is one thing all golfers have in common.

————

"I've always said basketball players are the greatest athletes in the world, but I think the golfers are the greatest professional performers because they have no teammates."

Sparky Anderson, 1990

"It is not necessarily the tallest, strongest, youngest, most athletic, or richest who wins."

Byron Nelson, 1946

"The guy who chokes least wins the most."

Hubert Green

"Every golfer is at heart a theorist."

Leslie Schon, 1923

"The more I practice, the luckier I seem to get."

Gary Player

"For the weekend player, golf is a game, something to enjoy during leisure time."

Rob Sauerhaft, 1991

"I dreamed one night that I had 17 holes-in-one and one two, and when I woke up I was so goddam mad."

Ben Hogan

"It is nothing new or original to say that golf is played one stroke at a time. But it took me many strokes to realize it."

Robert T. Jones, Jr.

"Golf is not a game of great shots. It's a game of most accurate misses. The people who win make the smallest mistakes."

Gene Littler

"For the most part, golfers don't have any teammates. Only opponents."

Peter McCleery, 1990

"I can play the game only one way. I must play every shot for all there is in it. I cannot play safe."

Robert T. Jones, Jr., 1921

"The woods are full of long hitters."

Jerry Barber

"Everyone cheats when they first start playing golf. A lot of people don't ever stop."

Frank Beard

"We all shoot better than we score."

Brian Swarbrick, 1972

"We all choke. You just try to choke least."

Tom Watson

"There is an adage in golf, for example, that nobody can beat anybody else if he cannot first conquer himself."

Charles Price, 1962

"Golf is an easy game for the beginner, because, as Mr. Lloyd George pointed out many years ago, it is the only game in the world in which the bad player gets the best of it."

Charles Whitcombe, 1949

"Without confidence a golfer is little more than a hacker."

Robert T. Jones, Jr., 1929

"If you have been able in 18 holes to hit one magnificent shot, you will have achieved a special kind of inside feeling."

Esteban Cardoza, senior golf
teacher at the Real Sociedad
Espanola Club de Campo in
Madrid, 1976

"The best golfers alive get into trouble now and then."

Don Herold, 1952

"Do not let us forget now and at all times that the game of golf is supported not by the scratch and professionals but by the ordinary moderate golfer of a handicap of about eight to 12. He is the backbone of the game and his enjoyment must be considered more than anybody else's."

Lord Brabazon of Tara,
1952

3

The Golfers

A few years ago, I read a very clever article by Frank Hannigan, then executive director of the USGA. It was a tongue-in-cheek interview with a new golfer who answered questions about the game with an extremely narrow view as to the history and tradition of the sport. One of the replies dealt with the origins of golf and the beginner replied that the game was introduced by Arnold Palmer and it was first developed for television.

There's a point here. Many current players have no knowledge of golf's history or its outstanding champions. Many people who have recently taken up the game, and who follow the results of tournaments on television or in newspapers and magazines, are probably more familiar with Wayne Levi than Francis Ouimet. Actually, if he wasn't participating on the Senior Tour, Arnold Palmer might be ancient history to the uninformed. Is it any wonder that the feats of Byron Nelson are all but forgotten? There have been so many wonderful golfers through the years, some of whom might be called great.

Offered here are brief sketches of some who particularly warrant being remembered.

ALLAN ROBERTSON—He was primarily a ball maker in the featherie period, depending on that trade to earn a living. Prior to his time golf professionals were mostly caddies. A St. Andrews native, he was considered the first true golf professional. It was popular to say he was never beaten in a match. Newspaper accounts of the period differ with that legend, although Robertson certainly had a great record in challenge matches. He will forever be remembered as the first golfer to ever break 80 at St. Andrews; we can only assume that was the 18-hole record for any course at that time. Robertson died in 1859, so he never played in the British Open. Some golfers alive at the time said the Open Championship was actually created to find a successor to Robertson, the man called simply, "champion golfer."

TOM MORRIS, SR.—More commonly called "Old Tom," Morris was an apprentice to Robertson at St. Andrews. A difference of opinion regarding the newly introduced gutta percha ball caused a split between the two with Morris moving to Prestwick. He was involved in many challenge matches, some as Robertson's partner, and together they were unbeatable. Old Tom won four Open Championships, an outstanding record, but he was not always given his proper due because of his son's prowess in the game.

TOM MORRIS, JR.—"Young Tom" was in a class by himself, winning his first Open at the age of 17. He followed that up with two more victories in succession and retired the Championship Belt. Thus, the championship was not held in 1871. The silver claret jug was then offered the following year and Tommy won his fourth straight title. However, the trophy was not yet available and while his name is the first engraved on it, Tommy never actually received it. All of his victories were accomplished in convincing style, far outdistancing the rest of the field. His wife died when he was only 24 and Morris died shortly after. In a very brief time, he became the greatest golfer in Scotland, which meant the greatest in the world.

JOHN BALL—In 1890, this golfer from the Liverpool area became the first Englishman as well as the first amateur to win the Open. He

Sr.

MORRIS

also holds the distinction of having won eight British Amateur titles, the highest total in any single major championship in history.

FREDDIE TAIT—Scotland needed a champion with the dominance of an Englishman and they found it in Freddie Tait. His record of two Amateur Championships could have been better had he not died in the Boer War at an early age.

HAROLD HILTON—Right on the heels of Ball came another English amateur who also played his golf at Hoylake. In addition to his four British Amateur titles, he won the British Open twice and the U.S. Amateur in 1911.

THE TRIUMVERATE—History has put James Braid, J. H. Taylor and Harry Vardon together because of their total dominance of golf. The three won a total of 16 British Opens, five each by Braid and Taylor with Vardon claiming six. Each was different, but each had the ability to play magnificent golf. Vardon was the stylist and best known. His exhibitions in America popularized golf on this side of the Atlantic, although a loss in the 1913 U.S. Open probably had even more effect, because of who won it.

FRANCIS OUIMET—He was a 20-year-old ex-caddie when he beat Vardon along with another English professional, Ted Ray, in a playoff for the 1913 U.S. Open. He would later win the U.S. Amateur twice, but it was that Open victory that endeared him to American golfers and would-be golfers. A true gentleman, Ouimet was highly regarded wherever golf was played and became the first American to serve as Captain of the Royal and Ancient Golf Club of St. Andrews.

JOHNNY McDERMOTT—Two years before Ouimet stunned the golf world, McDermott became the first American-born golfer to win the U.S. Open. Just to prove it was no fluke, he successfully defended his title in 1912. A proud ex-caddie from Philadelphia, he was afraid of no golfer and was willing to play anyone who wished to bet against him.

WALTER TRAVIS—He actually came on the scene before the two golfers previously mentioned and was America's first outstanding amateur although he was born in Australia. A three-time U.S. Amateur champion, he was the first "foreigner" to win the British Amateur. His putting played a major role in the victory, a fact taken seriously by the British. He used a center-shaft putter which became the subject of British ire and the R&A banned such putters. They were made legal just before Ben Hogan took the trip to Carnoustie and won the British Open using a center-shaft putter.

JEROME TRAVERS—One of only five amateurs to win the U.S. Open, he had several matches against Travis. He won the U.S. Amateur four times and most of the other important amateur events in America in his day.

CHARLES (CHICK) EVANS—Another amateur who won the U.S. Open, he set a scoring record in the 1916 championship while using only seven clubs. Twice a U.S. Amateur champion, he dominated the Western Amateur and eventually founded the most successful caddie scholarship program in the country for the Western Golf Association.

WALTER HAGEN—His record of 11 major championships is enough to consider The Haig as one of the all-time greats. It was his lifestyle, however, that set him apart. He raised the social standing of the professional golfer from that of a servant, especially in Britain, to that of a sought-after personality. He was equally at home with kings and caddies. To Hagen, money was something to be spent. When he won his first British Open, he endorsed the check over to his caddie. When he died, less than a third of his medals were found, most of them having been given to admiring fans, some of whom he had just met moments before. He was as popular as Babe Ruth, Red Grange and Jack Dempsey in the golden era of sports in the United States.

GENE SARAZEN—"The Squire" was the first golfer to win all four majors in which a professional could compete—U.S. Open, British Open, PGA Championship and the Masters. Only Ben Hogan, Jack

Nicklaus and Gary Player have been able to duplicate the feat. Sarazen hit what was perhaps the most famous shot in history, a four-wood for a double-eagle in the final round of the 1935 Masters, enabling him to tie Craig Wood and then win in a playoff.

ROBERT T. JONES, JR.—His friends called him Bob and the British affectionately called him Bobby. Some who revere his stature, refer to him as Mr. Jones. Until Nicklaus broke it, his 13 major championships stood as the record. Jones established his mark as a young man and he retired at age 28. When his competitive years were behind him, Jones was in demand to show his skills on film. His swing appears as classic and impeccable today as in the 1930s. Augusta National and the Masters Tournament will always be a living memorial to his greatness.

LEO DIEGEL—He was known as the professional of the stars after moving to California from his native Michigan. A two-time PGA champion, Diegel was a member of the first U.S. Ryder Cup team.

TOMMY ARMOUR—Few playing professionals can make the transition to teaching professional successfully, but that was the case with Armour. A Scot by birth, he made his name after emigrating to the United States. He won the U.S. Open, then followed that up with a PGA victory and the British Open. Many know him as the "Silver Scot" made famous by the golf clubs bearing that name. However, Armour was the "Black Scot" before his hair turned gray.

JOYCE WETHERED (LADY HEATHCOAT-AMORY)—She was the first of the great women golfers and was compared to Jones because of the style and grace of her swing. Beginning in 1920, she won five consecutive English Ladies championships and won four British women's titles in six attempts.

GLENNA COLLETT (VARE)—The American equivalent to Joyce Wethered, she is considered by many to be the best amateur player ever in the United States. In just 14 years, she won the U.S. women's championship six times, was runner-up twice and twice a semifinalist. She also won the North and South and the Eastern Amateur six times each.

LAWSON LITTLE—He is not remembered as well as some of the other amateurs, but his record in 1934 and 1935 holds a special place in golf history. He accomplished the "Little Slam" by winning the British and U.S. Amateurs in both years. After turning professional, he also captured the 1940 U.S. Open.

SIR T. HENRY COTTON—Unfortunately, Cotton died before he was knighted, although he was aware the honor was to be given to him by Queen Elizabeth II. He won three British Opens and was the shining star for Great Britain after the Americans began to dominate the game. Sir Henry was a Hagen-type and a proud man. He shot a 65 en route to winning his first Open and the Dunlop 65 golf ball was so named to honor that accomplishment.

ARTHUR D'ARCY (BOBBY) LOCKE—His detractors called him "Old Muffin Face," but they were mostly American professionals who were not used to being beaten by someone from South Africa. He was the first successful non-American on the PGA Tour and was virtually banned from playing in the United States. He won four British Opens along with many tournaments world-wide. His putting skill was second to none.

BYRON NELSON—Many of his accomplishments have not received the proper honor, because his two greatest years were in 1944 and 1945 when many golfers were in the armed forces. That's unfortunate, as Lord Byron was one of the finest golfers to ever play the game. He won the Masters, U.S. Open and PGA before the war against the likes of Hogan, Snead, Demaret, Guhldahl and Wood, all winners of majors. In 1945 he won 11 consecutive tournaments on the PGA Tour and 18 events in total. His real aim was to buy a ranch in his native Texas—a goal he achieved following his magnificent 1945 season.

SAM SNEAD—He came from West Virginia and startled the golf world with the sweetest swing ever seen. He, too, is at times overlooked as one of the greats of all time since he never won the U.S. Open. But, he need not apologize with a record of three Masters, three PGA Championships, a British Open and 84 official Tour titles.

The Senior Tour came along a little too late for Sam as he was competing on the regular Tour in his 60's. He was the first and only golfer to shoot his age on the PGA Tour and with the seniors now competing with their own after the age of 50, may well end up as the only golfer ever to do so.

BEN HOGAN—At first they called him "Bantam Ben." He rifled tee shots out with the longest hitters, but it was for his accomplishments later in his career that everyone remembers him. He placed shots like no one before him so that he was in the best position to approach the green or putt to the hole. He practiced more than anyone and the result was golf that simply was the best and earned him status as a legend.

JIMMY DEMARET—While other golfers were playing in white shirts and ties, Demaret introduced every color in the rainbow in his outfits. A lesser man couldn't have pulled it off, but he had the game to match. He was the first to win three Masters titles. Jimmy enjoyed life as Hagen before him and probably would have won many more tournaments had he been more serious.

MILDRED (BABE) ZAHARIAS—The Babe changed women's golf. She was an excellent athlete, having won gold medals in the Olympics before turning her attention to golf. After becoming the first American to win the British title, she turned professional and pretty much dominated the early Tour. She won three U.S. Women's Opens along with a host of other tournaments.

PETER THOMSON—Before Thomson became a world golfer, there were other Australians who had made their mark—like Joe Kirkwood, Jim Ferrier and Norman von Nida—but not in the manner of Thomson. He won five British Opens along with titles on every part of the globe.

Thomson didn't much care for the PGA Tour, but did come back and win on the Senior Tour.

Australia has had many outstanding golfers. In addition to those previously mentioned, there have been Kel Nagle, Bruce Devlin, Bruce Crampton, Graham Marsh, David Graham, Greg Norman and most recently Wayne Grady, the 1990 PGA champion.

MARY KATHRYN (MICKEY) WRIGHT—Mickey was a combination of Byron Nelson when it came to winning consecutive tournaments and Sam Snead if the discussion gets around to the best golf swings. She completely dominated the LPGA Tour in the early 1960s, won four U.S. Women's Opens and four LPGA Championships. Whenever the subject of the greatest woman golfer arises, Mickey is right at the top of the list and rightfully so.

BILLY CASPER—The "Big Three" in the 1960s consisted of Palmer, Player and Nicklaus. It should have been the "Big Four" with the addition of Casper. Like many of the great putters in history, Casper seemed to be overlooked as a golfer, as if putting wasn't a part of the game. That's too bad, because even the best putters can't capitalize on their specialty unless they first get the ball on the green in a reasonable number of strokes. He was twice the U.S. Open champion and also won the Masters in addition to many Tour titles.

ARNOLD PALMER—Few golfers in history have captured the imagination of fans as has Palmer. His slashing style has, in a large part, been responsible for his following. Of course, the record had to be there as well or interest would have ebbed rapidly. Four Masters, two British Opens, a U.S. Amateur and the 1960 U.S. Open are the majors in Palmer's list of victories. In addition to his titles and personality, notable contributions were made by Arnold by playing in the British Open. His participation elevated the stature of that oldest of championships, permitting it once again to attract the best golfers in the world.

GARY PLAYER—If anyone in the game deserves the title of "World Golfer," it's Player. While small of stature, he not only worked on his game, but his strength to make himself competitive in tournament golf. He did more than that. His determination lifted him to the top. Except for the U.S. Open, which he won in 1965, Gary has won every other major at least twice. He has won on every continent on which competitive golf is played and was the most successful non-American on both the regular and senior tours, all of this while accumulating more mileage than a full-time pilot for Pan Am.

JACK NICKLAUS—His record in the majors is the best in history. Among his majors, he has won more Masters (six) than any golfer and Jack's five PGA Championships and four U.S. Opens are equal to the record. In the hallowed halls of golf's legends, Nicklaus has his own wing.

LEE TREVINO—"Super Mex" was a breath of fresh air when he joined the Tour. While Sam Snead may have had the classic swing, Trevino had one which became the most recognizable and efficient. He won the British Open, U.S. Open and PGA twice. Only his failure to capture the Masters remains as a blemish. Lee was convinced that Augusta National was built for a right-to-left player and never played well there.

TOM WATSON—It's funny that Jack Nicklaus was unliked in some circles because he came along and beat the reigning king, Arnold Palmer. Watson almost faced the same kind of treatment when he came along and beat Nicklaus, who had gained the admiration and respect of the golfing public. His eight major victories, Vardon Trophies and Player of the Year awards are enough to include him among the best of all time and he's a gentleman on and off the course.

THE GOLFERS

"Every generation swears that its sporting heroes and heroines are better than any before or since."

Enid Wilson, 1952

"A man may be the best player and still he cannot win the championship unless the luck be with him."

Bernard Darwin, 1931

"Every great golfer has learned to think positively, to assume the success and not the failure of a shot, to disregard misfortune and to accept disaster, and never to indulge the futility of remorse or blame."

Pat Ward-Thomas, 1961

"I have always felt and said that a man who can be a champion in one era could be a champion in any other era because he has what it takes to reach the top."

Ben Hogan

"To qualify as a truly great golfer in my mind is to establish standards, using native talent with a hard-earned technique peculiarly a man's own, all taken for what it's worth within the context of his own times."

Charles Price, 1979

"To compare the 'greats' of different generations in any sport is a pointless task."

James K. Robertson, 1967

"No great golfer underestimates the game, the course, or the opposition."

Pat Ward-Thomas, 1961

"In golf, the best players prefer the strongest tests, where skill is most readily rewarded, inferior play is promptly penalized, and the gap between the best and the mediocre is widened."

Joseph C. Dey, Jr.

"It is impossible to compare performances of one generation with those of another. It is enough to say that talent begets talent, but genius is unique."

Louis T. Stanley

"Comparisons between players of different generations are, as a rule, futile, and particularly so in the case of golf, since the conditions under which it is played have so greatly changed."

Bernard Darwin, 1937

"Greatness is not achieved simply by striking the ball supremely well, but by doing so when it matters most."

Pat Ward-Thomas, 1961

WALTER HAGEN

"His golf exactly matched his personality. Often brilliant; never, never dull."

Henry Longhurst

"He etched his personality so deeply on the minds of sports followers that the mere mention of his name still evokes the full image of the man—hair brilliantined, face tanned and smiling with an almost Oriental inscrutability, clothes that would have looked showy on anyone else, the haughty stride back onto the brambles and onto the carpet. This man, you felt, had always been that way. Like Athena, he had undoubtedly emerged full-blown from the forehead of some 20th-Century Zeus."

Herbert Warren Wind

"Hagen was the first professional to make a million dollars at the game—and the first to spend it."

Fred Corcoran

"I think he was, without question, the greatest putter of all time. He could putt any kind of green under any conditions."

Gene Sarazen, 1975

"His golf was fallible and impertinent, which endeared him to the common man."

Henry Longhurst

"Walter Hagen was the greatest loser and the greatest winner and the greatest golfer."

Chick Evans, 1969

"Walter Hagen was there when it all began in 1916 and, through the years, his loyalty and affection for his fellow professionals in the PGA of America never wavered or became diluted. From the beginning to the very end, The Haig considered himself no more nor less than a staunch member of our association committed to its principles, and sharing a common destiny with the youngest shop assistant in the game. That is what was so wonderful about The Haig. He was a professional's professional."

> Leo Fraser, president of the
> PGA of America, 1969

"Walter Hagen had a sterling contempt for second place. He believed that the public only remembered the winner, that a man might as well be 10th as second when the shooting was over."

> Herbert Warren Wind

"Sir Walter Hagen was the greatest golfer that ever lived. I truly believe this, greater than even Vardon and Vardon went three and one-half years without hitting a sandtrap."

> Wilfrid Reid, 1953

"Hagen seems to have all that is necessary for championship golf since he does the right thing at the right time. I predict he'll win our championship not once, but several times."

> Harry Vardon, 1920 (Hagen
> did go on to win four British
> Opens)

"Making a million or having the return of his laundry delayed by fiscal factors, nothing bothers Hagen. He could relax sitting on a hot stove."

> Tommy Armour, 1935

HAGEN

"Walter Hagen will always be one of the great names in the world of golf. He was a colorful and competent competitor and an admirable sportsman. I am thankful that I had many opportunities to play with him in championship competition. I have been asked for an anecdote about Hagen. I knew him so well and knew so much about him that it is impossible to select one episode of more interest than others. I think it is enough to say that his contribution to the game will always be remembered. I respected him in life and will revere his memory."

Robert T. Jones, Jr., 1969

"My son Walter will probably win it. He usually does,"

William Hagen, answering a
reporter's question at
Midlothian, 1939

"Decidely unorthodox and a suggestion of a sway, but I am going to reserve my decision on this chap until I have seen more of his game. After all, he appears to have the fundamentals; and a lad with a stout heart can come nearer to scoring than the perfect golfing robot without a heart."

Harry Vardon, after his first
look at Hagen's game, 1920

"Golf has never had a showman like him. All the professionals who have a chance to go after the big money today should say a silent thanks to Walter each time they stretch a check between their fingers. It was Walter who made professional golf what it is."

Gene Sarazen, 1950

"He was the finest short-iron player the game has ever known. He was a magnificent putter. He had the courage and unquestioning faith in himself."

Gene Sarazen, 1950

"He hits the ball lower through the wind; he can stand stiller on the green than any of them; when it comes to getting out of trouble he is without a peer."

Bernard Darwin, 1929

"He is willing to believe all shots cannot be played perfectly, and though he does play most of them faultlessly, a ragged stretch of golf will not dampen his ardor, for he thinks in the end all things are evened up."

Francis Ouimet, 1923

"A great golfer, Hagen. The greatest match player the world has ever seen, and we don't mean perhaps."

William Richardson, 1927

"He had such a way with him that crowds were ready to watch him when he had not the remotest chance of winning."

Bernard Darwin, 1944

"I love to play with Walter. He goes along chin up, smiling away; never grousing about his luck, playing the ball as he finds it. He can come nearer beating luck itself than anybody I know."

Robert T. Jones, Jr.

"Walter Hagen is proverbially a fine sportsman; a courteous opponent; a good loser, when he loses. He never kicks about his luck; he takes the breaks as they come."

O. B. Keeler, 1923

"Walter Hagen was the most spectacular figure who ever played golf."

Bob Harlow

"He was certainly no great stylist and swayed forward considerably as he came on to the ball, this probably being the cause of him hitting, and expecting to hit, a number of downright bad shots every round."

Henry Longhurst

"He was at once happy-go-lucky and casual, and yet shrewd, observant, and resolute."

Charles Mortimer, 1952

"He had that magnetism, the electric quality, that fired the imagination. He lived the life lesser men dream about as they plod back and forth every day between their offices and the subway."

Fred Corcoran

"There is no doubt that Hagen is the greatest artist that golf has produced."

Bob Harlow, 1929

"Hagen played in tournaments as though they were cocktail parties."

Charles Price, 1979

"Walter Hagen used to beat people on sheer gall. The same gall that let him walk in the front door of clubhouses without wiping his feet."

Jim Murray, 1978

"Hagen became a legend in his lifetime and if some of the stories that will forever be told of him are apocryphal, they pass muster because they so easily might have been true."

Henry Longhurst, 1952

"I do not know a better man around the greens than Walter."

Robert T. Jones, Jr.

"Walter Hagen goes down in history as the greatest exponent of the dramatic art of turning three shots into two."

Henry Longhurst

"Walter Hagen was also a master clubmaker. He had a touch and eyes that made a club a precision instrument."

Herb Graffis

"The Haig was the first great professional in American golf."

Charles Price, 1966

"Walter Hagen never knew where his ball was going and he had to invent six or seven new shots every time he played just to get his ball back into play."

Peter Dobereiner, 1990

"I feel that swashbuckling Walter Hagen was the outstandingly pictur- esque character of them all—the top philosopher and the greatest funster of the lot—and no mean golfer, to boot."

Don Herold, 1952

"The Haig was the first athlete in history to earn a million dollars. For a time he made more money than Babe Ruth, but he spent more than the entire Yankee outfield."

Charles Price, 1966

"He was one of the great, great men in our sport. Not only was he known as the King of the Fairways, but he was also saluted as the King of the Clubhouse."

Tommy Bolt

"Hagen overwhelmed his adversary by the sheer impetuosity of his at- tack."

Robert H. K. Browning, 1955

"He was a golfer of so many parts that one cannot catalogue them all. But they all added up to one thing—greatness."

Tom Scott

"Hagen was colorful, eccentric, theatrical, gregarious. He loved wine and women and his fellow men, from caddies to Princes of Wales, and saw no reason why life should not permanently be standing him a bottle of champagne."

Henry Longhurst

"Hagen had style. He demanded the best clothes. Even on the course his shirts were silk, and his plus-fours immaculately pressed with creases down the sides."

Michael McDonnell

"For all his knightliness he was always human—and he still is."

Harry Le Duc,
The Detroit News, 1952

"Walter Hagen remains the master of golf's thrills. He is the dramatist of the game, the leading actor, the most colorful of all golfers, amateur or professional."

H. G. Salsinger,
The Detroit News, 1929

"Whenever he played he simply oozed with the joy of life. The more he was up against it the better he played."

Percy Boomer

"Hagen was the match-play king and that goes for all time. He had no equal when it was man-to-man."

Grantland Rice, 1952

"Hagen was a flamboyant character who gave the sport style and sophistication."

Michael McDonnell, 1982

"As long as I've known Hagen—40 years—I've found him without inhibitions of any sort. Whether he's with the King of England or a broken-down caddie, Hagen has never changed his manner to suit the occasion."

Grantland Rice, 1952

"He's in golf to live, not to make a living."

Chick Evans

THE TRIUMVIRATE

"Vardon played as if he were enjoying the game, Braid as if he were going through his day's work, and Taylor, in certain moods at any rate, as if he hated it."

Bernard Darwin

HARRY VARDON

"I could say a lot about Harry Vardon, but why give praise where it is not needed."

Andra Kirkaldy

"Vardon always played well within himself. He always kept 10 yards of his power in reserve and there were times, when he hit the ball flat out, that he could add as much as 30 yards to a drive."

Gene Sarazen

"With Vardon came a style so effortless and simple that it seemed the most logical thing in the world to imitate rather than to hobble along with one's own eccentricities."

Charles Price, 1962

Taylor

Braid

VARDON

"In his early days Harry Vardon had a most ungainly style."

J. H. Taylor

"As big and powerful as Harry Vardon was his shots seldom displayed his power. He was a smart golfer—one of the very smartest the game has ever known."

Tommy Armour, 1959

"If a dog crossed the tee in front of him while at the top of his swing, he would be able to judge whether the dog ran in any danger of its life. If it did, he would stop his club; if it didn't, he would go through with the shot, without pulling or slicing."

Andra Kirkaldy

"I do not think anyone who saw him in his prime will disagree as to this, that a greater golfing genius is inconceivable."

Bernard Darwin

"Apart from his personal skill and prowess, Vardon molded the golfing technique not only of the British but also the world."

Tom Scott

"For all his superior style, he was probably the worst putter of his era."

Michael McDonnell

"It is to Vardon's everlasting credit that so free was his game of any weakness—excepting a tendency late in his career to jab short putts—that it was conversely never known for any particular strength. His whole game was strong."

                                                                        Charles Price, 1962

"They all say that Harry Vardon introduced it (the Vardon grip) but that's not fact. My father never gripped the club any other way. The rest of the players of the time were using the palm grip—rather like the baseball style."

                                                                        Jack Taylor,
                                                                        son of J. H. Taylor

"Vardon gets distance by the tremendous rapidity with which he makes the club travel through the air in the last few feet before the head reaches the ball, and this he does with his wrists only, which are exceptionally strong."

                                                                        Charles Cox

"He did what only a great golfer can do; he raised the general conception of what was possible in his game and forced his nearest rivals to attain a higher standard by attempting that which they would otherwise have deemed impossible."

                                                                        Bernard Darwin, 1937

"Harry Vardon was an utterly natural golfer. He never asked anyone to give him a lesson and nobody ever had the audacity to offer him one."

                                                                        Charles Price

"He was not only immensely long with the iron clubs, but a master of every kind of shorter iron shot, and before his illness he was not, whatever he may have been after it, a bad putter."

Bernard Darwin

"Vardon was great because he was the type of player who could adapt himself to all conditions and all courses. He was the only champion I can think of who was not an excellent putter."

Gene Sarazen

"He was a cautious, shy man who nevertheless earned a public following as great as any theatrical performer of his day and his money matches attracted thousands of spectators."

Michael McDonnell, 1982

Harry Vardon and John Ball

"Both had the killer instinct but with this difference. Vardon smiled during the process whilst Johnnie set about the job gloomily silent and apparently contemptuous as if pitying the unfortunate who was opposing him."

J. H. Taylor

John Ball

"I claim that Johnny Ball is the best amateur that has ever been seen, for a match. It did not need that he would win the Open Championship and the Amateur Championship eight times, in order to prove this."

Horace Hutchinson, 1919

"He has become in his lifetime a figure of legend."

Bernard Darwin

"Some allowance must be made to the hero-worshipper, and I can only say that I would rather watch Mr. Ball play than any other man, and that of all the beautiful styles his had for me a beauty apart."

Bernard Darwin

"I have never seen a player whose hitting was such a pleasure to watch, such a beautiful exhibition of grace and power."

Horace Hutchinson, 1900

"His swing was the true poetry of motion, the most perfectly smooth and rhythmical imaginable."

Bernard Darwin, 1952

ROBERT T. JONES, JR.

"Little Bobby Jones of Atlanta is a really fine player, and shows every indication of becoming a tremendously great one, once he is master of himself, which must come with maturity."

A. W. Tillinghast, 1916
(when Jones was only 14)

"Bobby Jones was the greatest championship golfer in history. That is more than just my opinion, it is a flat fact."

Charles Price, 1980

"It is nonsense to talk about who was the greatest golfer in the world. All you can see that there have been none greater than Bobby Jones."

Tommy Armour

"He began the downswing almost as a continuance of the upswing, with no perceptible break in rhythm, and accelerated smoothly to the point of impact and beyond."

Tom Scott

"One of the great champions that ever lived, he will be remembered as much for his qualities as a person as for his transcending skill at golf, and this in its time was beyond compare."

Pat Ward-Thomas

"Jones was the most genuinely modest person I have ever met. When one had talked with him for a short time he gave you the feeling that the only difference between your golf and his was that he had been much more lucky."

Raymond Oppenheimer, a
British amateur paired with
Jones in first two rounds of the
1930 British Open

"No one before or since him has played the game with more modesty, thoughtfulness and integrity."

Charles Price

"I think he is the greatest golfer I ever saw."

Patty Berg, 1937

JONES

"The most remarkable thing about Mr. Jones seems to me to be this, that he can win an Open championship without playing really well."

Bernard Darwin, 1930

"Of all the people I've met in sports—or out—Jones came the closest to being what we call a great man. He had the quality of being at the same time much larger than life and exceedingly human."

Herbert Warren Wind

"I have found only one sports figure who could stand up in every way as a gentleman as well as a celebrity, a fine, decent human being as well as a newsprint personage, and one who has never once since I have known him let me down in my estimate of him."

Paul Gallico

"There was a clear, cold aesthetic thrill in watching Jones hit a golf ball."

Herbert Warren Wind

"It's a shame, but he'll never make a golfer . . . too much temper."

Alex Smith, 1915

"This kid will be one of the world's greatest in a few more years."

Jim Barnes, 1915

"He can never improve his shots if that's what you mean. But he will learn a great deal more about playing them. And his putting is faulty."

Walter Travis, after seeing
Jones play in his first
U.S. Amateur in 1916

"Bobby was playing some good golf in spots. He's got everything he needs to win any championship, except experience—and maybe philosophy. But I'll tip you off to something—Bobby will win an Open before he wins an Amateur."

> Walter Hagen, 1921 (Jones
> won the 1923 U.S. Open, his
> first major title)

"He is now what Harry Vardon was at his very best—the greatest golfer in the world."

> Bobby Cruickshank, 1923

"So natural, so effortless, so subtly beautiful is his golf swing that an observer is conscious only of the utter rightness of the method."

> Carlton Wells, 1925

"Bob was a fine man to be partnered with in a tournament. Congenial and considerate, he made you feel you were playing with a friend, and you were."

> Gene Sarazen

"With no formal golf training, Jones' technique was completely natural."

> Michael McDonnell, 1982

"For a little man like me to receive this greatest award in golf makes me feel 10 feet tall. I don't know why they picked me for this award. If I were half the man Bobby Jones was, I'd be higher than the Empire State Building."

> Chi Chi Rodriguez, upon
> being presented the
> Bob Jones Award, 1989

"He combined exquisite artistry with utterly relentless precision in a way not quite given to other golfers. Just to see him swing a club was a joy."

Bernard Darwin

"Jones was not only a good golfer but a beautiful one, an artist where others were mere craftsmen, with a style steeped in rhythm and form."

Al Laney

"With dignity he quit the scene on which he nothing common did."

New York Times editorial
when Jones announced his
retirement from tournament
golf, 1930

LAWSON LITTLE

"Like many big, solid men, Little had a velvet touch on the greens, and when this and his long game were working at their best, he was probably, with the exception of Jones himself, the most formidable amateur golfer the game has seen."

Henry Longhurst, 1952

"He never choked in his life. Never once did he lose a tournament he was leading. Never."

Jack Burke, Jr.

JAMES BRAID

"To this day Braid remains one of the greatest golfing figures of all time. Calm and inperturable, he will go down in history for some outstanding records achieved within a remarkable short space of time."

Peter Alliss, 1988

"Braid has a drive of amazing power, but nobody could call it one of supreme elegance. His style is powerful, but slovenly, and when he draws back his club before hitting, you ask yourself if Braid really has all the mastery desirable over his weapon."

Horace Hutchinson

"Certainly he was capable of errors which Vardon and Taylor could hardly have made, but his powers of recovery were immense; not merely could he move mountains by sheer strength but he was master of every kind of shot, delicate or ferocious, when in trouble, in particular the 'explosion' shot from a bunker near the pin."

Bernard Darwin

"I have yet to meet the player who could hole the 10-yard putts with greater regularity."

J. H. Taylor

"James was a terrific driver and there was no finer iron player alive; in temperament he was resolute, patient and imperturbable."

Bernard Darwin, 1952

"Braid is indeed the embodiment of what every golfer should wish to be, both on the links and off them."

Lord Simon, at a celebration
of Braid's 80th birthday

"He was a man of exceptional power and could impart a 'divine fury' to many of his strokes."

Charles Mortimer, 1952

"A prince of sportsmen."

Andra Kirkaldy

John Henry Taylor

"Taylor played an important part in raising the standards of professional golf and was largely responsible for the formation of the Professional Golfers' Association in 1901."

Peter Alliss, 1988

"There was a noteworthy sameness in his method of playing all his strokes, and it seemed to make of golf a game of almost monotonous simplicity."

Bernard Darwin, 1952

"One of the best English professionals of our time, he possesses one of the shortest swings I have ever seen."

Arnaud Massy, 1911

"Taylor's great strength is in his approach play."

Horace Hutchinson

"His control of the driver was mystifying in its deadly accuracy. Before teeing off he would designate to us where the best place to aim in anticipation of the second shot and would then proceed to drop his own ball there for an absolute bull's eye."

Jerome Travers

"When he pulled down his cap, stuck out his chin, and embedded his large boots in the ground, he could hit straight through the wind as if it were not there, and I think the finest golf I ever saw was his at Hoylake in 1913."

Bernard Darwin

ALLAN ROBERTSON

"His style was neat and effective. He held his clubs at the end of the handle, even his putter high up. His clubs were light and his stroke an easy, swift switch. With him the game was as much of head as of hand. He always kept cool, and generally pulled through a match even when he got behind. He was a natural gentleman, honourable and true."

James Balfour, 1887

"Allan Robertson was the most outstanding figure and the most interesting figure on any links in the first half of the 19th Century."

W. W. Tulloch

"Much was written about Allan Robertson as a player. The claims are far from modest, and may be exaggerated, but he was unquestionably a fine golfer."

Louis T. Stanley

"He was a wizard with the cleek. He was the pioneer of precision iron play."

                                             Will Grimsley, 1966

"Allan Robertson will go down in golf history as the first of the great professional players."

                                             Peter Alliss, 1988

"Allan Robertson was obviously a player of great skill and of an easy and beautiful style, but also obviously he lacked power compared with his rivals."

                                             Bernard Darwin, 1952

"They may shut up their shops and toll their bells, for the greatest among them is gone."

                                             A member of the
                                             Royal and Ancient, upon
                                             Robertson's death in 1859

"The cunningest bit body o' a player that ever handled club, cleek or putter."

                                             Tom Morris, Sr.

"Allan Robertson, the greatest golf-player that ever lived, of whom alone in the annals of the pastime it can be said that he never was beaten."

                                             Dundee Advertiser, 1859

"It is clear that Allan was an unsurpassed artist at the game, but that he was never beaten, as is alleged, was partly due to the fact that he refused to run the risk."

Bernard Darwin, 1952

HAROLD HILTON

"I have never known anyone who knew so much about the game or who had such powers of observation in regard to it."

Bernard Darwin

"Hilton lunged at the ball and was walking as part of the follow-through."

Michael McDonnell

"There have been greater hitters of the ball than Harold, though very, very few, and they were so simply, I think, because they had greater physical advantages. There have been, in my judgement, none who knew the game as well as he did,"

Bernard Darwin

"Although he was only 5 feet 7 inches tall, his power belied his size and made him a giant of British golf in the days of such great professionals as Braid, Taylor and Vardon."

Peter Alliss, 1988

"Till Bobby Jones appeared, it might safely be said of him that Mr. Hilton was the greatest of all amateur score players."

Bernard Darwin, 1933

TOM MORRIS, SR.

"By far the best-known Scottish figure in the emergent days of golf was Old Tom Morris whose 87 years of life spanning from 1821 to 1908, mark the most vital epoch in the game and the golden era for St. Andrews."

James K. Robertson, 1967

"Old Tom lived to become an institution; he was the veritable Nestor of golf—with his long life, his vast stories of experience, tradition and golfing lore."

Charles Mortimer, 1952

"The High Priest of the Hierarchy of Professional Golf."

Horace Hutchinson

"To generations of people all over the world his name and his picture epitomized golf."

James K. Robertson, 1967

"His own way was, in his sheer terror of missing the putt, to get done with it as quickly as possible, and often he would just go up to the ball and hit it in a nervous hurry, without looking at the line at all, so that he hardly gave himself a ghost of a chance of holing."

Horace Hutchinson, 1919

"As a player himself, he never earned the fame that was Allan Robertson's before him, yet Tom Morris was four times Open champion and had, on occasion, beaten Robertson."

James K. Robertson, 1967

TOM MORRIS, JR.

"Without doubt, 'Young Tom' Morris was the greatest golfer in the early days of championship golf."

Peter Alliss, 1988

"He was without peer among them all."

Charles Blair Macdonald,
1928

"Without doubt he was the finest golfer of his time."

Louis T. Stanley

"He was a slasher; by temperment not 'douse' nor canny after Allan Robertson's pattern, but a bold spirit, trying for long carries."

Horace Hutchinson

"Young Tommy was perhaps the best player that ever appeared on the green. He was a tall, handsome athlete, and unmatched at all parts of the game."

James Balfour, 1887

"I could cope with Allan masel' but never wi' Tommy."

Tom Morris, Sr.

"Suffice to leave it that 'Young Tom' was peerless in his day."

James K. Robertson, 1967

"No golfer of today, except it be Bobby Jones, is the equal of young Tom Morris."

Charles Blair Macdonald,
1928

"We must assign him a place in the small company of very great golfers."

Charles Darwin, 1952

"I can't imagine anyone playing better than Tommy."

Leslie Balfour

FREDDIE TAIT

"He reveled in the cut-and-thrust of match play and the rapidly growing galleries of the time loved him for it, and for his high spirits."

James K. Robertson, 1967

"Had he survived to the rubber-core era he would have been, one may venture to say, almost more terrible than before, for the new ball would have suited to perfection that controlled method of his and his skill in every kind of running shot."

Bernard Darwin

"Freddie Tait was the very keenest golfer, as a boy, that I ever saw. I had watched him at St. Andrews, growing up from a small boy's to a young man's estate, and acquiring the mastery of his clubs as he grew. He was a favorite with everybody."

Horace Hutchinson

"On my own green, by an amateur! It's no possible, but it's a fact!"
Ben Sayers, North Berwick
professional after losing to Tait
on his home course by eight
holes

"He was always supposed to be a lucky player, and I think this was in his case a very high compliment, because the player who is thought lucky is always courageous, and Freddie Tait's golf was full of courage."
Bernard Darwin

"Frederick Guthrie Tait should be remembered as St. Andrews' and Scotland's greatest amateur."
Louis T. Stanley

GENE SARAZEN

"Famous for his plus-fours as well as for his bunker shots, Gene Sarazen was one of the giants of golf."
Peter Alliss, 1988

"Whether he was winning or losing, coming close or straggling back in the pack, Gene Sarazen has always been an enchanting player to watch and one of the sport's most attractive personalities."
Herbert Warren Wind

"The name speaks for itself. He stands for all the good there is in golf."
Jimmy Demaret

"I know of no other golfer who plays the game so firmly and yet who touches up his play with such grace."

                                                                    Chick Evans

"I shall not attempt to rate the golfers in the field when I was playing in top form. I'll just say that at one time or another they all gave me trouble. But Gene Sarazen seemed to give me the most, despite the nine more years of experience I had."

                                                        Walter Hagen, 1957

"Gene Sarazen was the simplest golfer I ever saw. He stood with both feet rooted to the ground, clasped the club firmly in both hands with a couple of inches of shaft showing at the top, and gave the ball a tremendous, elementary thump."

                                                            Henry Longhurst

"He was cocky and self-confident, but he had plenty of moxie and determination and could concentrate solidly on his game."

                                                               Walter Hagen

WALTER TRAVIS

"In many respects Walter J. Travis will stand as the most remarkable golfer that ever lived. Just consider, as a starter, these two facts. He won the first tournament he ever entered at the age of 35, a month or so after he had hit his first golf ball. He won the last tournament he ever entered, the Metropolitan Championship, at the age of 54, in 1915 and on his way through he beat Jerry Travers, the United States Open champion of the same year."

                                                              Grantland Rice

"No man in America ever worked so hard to become a great golfer as he did, and as his reward he has won the amateur championship of the United States three times and the British amateur championship once."

Jerome Travers, 1913

"Now see, Horace, that you don't get beaten by that American."

Bobby Maxwell to Horace
Hutchinson when the latter
beat Maxwell in the British
Amateur, 1904 (Travis beat
him in the semi-final match)

"Put him down at 180 or any less number of yards from the hole and there was no player, amateur or professional, better than he. Perhaps there was no amateur as good."

Horace Hutchinson, 1919

"He was one of the steadiest golfers I had ever seen—a man of fine judgement and marvelous exactness, who always played with his head and was constantly giving the closest possible study to the game."

Harry Vardon, 1922

"He had not begun his game young, he was essentially a made player, he was gifted with no great power, although he had always a little something up his sleeve; but he had drilled himself into great accuracy of striking: he had a fine, hostile, match-playing temperament and he was a supremely good putter."

Bernard Darwin, 1952

"I never hit a careless shot in my life. I bet only a quarter but I play each shot as if it was for the title."

Walter Travis

"Walter Travis was one of those men who saw no sense in doing a thing at all unless he did it well."

Herbert Warren Wind

JEROME TRAVERS

"Travers rates as one of the greatest competitors who ever played any game. He had Ben Hogan's concentration."

Grantland Rice, 1954

"He was a courageous golfer and never knew when he was beaten."

Francis Ouimet, 1931

"He was totally lacking in what today we call charisma."

Jess Sweetser

"The most serious, unsmiling golfer I ever caddied for. And he was the only golfer at the club who did not play for money."

Mike Cestone, his caddie at
Montclair Country Club

"Travers was the greatest competitor I have ever known."

Alex Smith

"The coldest, hardest golfer I ever knew."

Chick Evans

"He was the best match player in the country."

Francis Ouimet

"I shall always think that the best putter I ever did see was Jerome Travers."

Bernard Darwin

Francis Ouimet

"No more popular golfer has ever come out of America."

Bernard Darwin, 1931

"Ouimet made that first big dent into the sports consciousness of America."

Grantland Rice, 1954

"With Francis Ouimet golf has always been a game."

Richard S. Tufts, 1962

"Francis was solemn as a judge; he always is in a match."

Robert T. Jones, Jr.

"Francis Ouimet was just about the nicest gentleman I ever knew."

Henry Longhurst

JESS SWEETSER

"Our Amateur Championship has gone to a citizen of the United States. There is no doubt that the best man won. Mr. Sweetser is armed with every possible stroke a golfer should have. I hope he will come back and defend his title and I hope we will beat him. My lords, ladies and gentlemen, are we downhearted?"

> **Captain S. Gillen,** of the Honourable Company of Edinburgh Golfers, at the presentation ceremonies, 1926

GEORGE VON ELM

"You can't expect anyone to go on beating as fine a golfer as Von Elm."

> **Robert T. Jones, Jr.** at the U.S. Amateur presentation ceremonies after Von Elm defeated Jones, 1926 (Jones had eliminated Von Elm from the championship the previous two years.)

ARNAUD MASSY

"Massy was beyond all question a grand golfer and a splendid figure of a man."

> **Bernard Darwin**

JOHNNY McDERMOTT

"I have never seen a man who, when called upon to hit a ball a given number of yards, could do so with such damned, irritating consistency."

> **Ted Ray**

"He was willing to wager on his ability to outplay any golfer in the world—Vardon not excepted—any time, any place, and for any amount of money."

                                                            Herbert Warren Wind

"McDermott would wager any amount on himself in practically any match he played. The fire of his own intensity burned out the little fellow and following that 1913 Open, McDermott went mentally astray and vanished into a home."

                                                            Grantland Rice, 1954

Joyce Wethered

"I was impressed more forcibly by her remarkable temperament under fire than by her invincible playing."

                                                            Glenna Collett

"Miss Wethered brought power combined with a perfection of style and a hitherto unknown degree of accuracy."

                                                            Enid Wilson

"In my era, Joyce Wethered was the greatest woman golfer."

                                                            Glenna Collett Vare, 1989

Glenna Collett Vare

"Her accuracy with the spoon and brassie is to me the most impressive part of her well-rounded game."

                                                            Robert T. Jones, Jr.

"Glenna was the finest woman golfer in this country that I ever saw."
Joseph C. Dey, Jr.

"Shy and modest to the point of being almost retiring, this charming young lady was the first of her sex to prove that women could hit the golf ball rather than sweep it."
Richard S. Tufts, 1962

"She was particularly good coming out of a trap, but actually she had all the shots."
Virginia Van Wie

ALEX SMITH

"Alex Smith not only was one of the pioneer Scottish professionals in this country, but is by all odds the most whimsical character."
Glenna Collett

JIM BARNES

"He is a player of exceptional ability, one of the closest students of form and style and the right way golf has, and with this he is one of the best instructors to be found in any golfing country."
Grantland Rice, 1925

"You ought to be good, you have a firm foundation."
James G. Harding,
presenting Barnes with the
trophy for winning the
U.S. Open and referring to his
large feet, 1921

CHARLES "CHICK" EVANS

"So solid was the swing he built that he was able to compete in every U.S. Amateur championship held between 1907 and 1962."

Al Barkow, 1980

MACDONALD SMITH

"Macdonald Smith was a golfer of a very different and a higher class, one who deserves serious consideration for the depressing honour of being the best player who never won a championship."

Bernard Darwin, 1944

T. HENRY COTTON

"Few people who know about golf would deny that Henry Cotton is the greatest golfer that Britain has produced this century."

Tom Scott

"He remains one of the very, very few people with whom I would sit up all night talking golf."

Henry Longhurst, 1952

TOMMY ARMOUR

"Tommy Armour had to overcome a tremendous physical handicap to become one of the most outstanding golfers in the period between the two world wars."

Peter Alliss, 1988

"The best pair of hands in American golf."

Gene Sarazen

"Not every great golfer becomes a renowned teacher, but Tommy Armour is one of those who has achieved great distinction in both spheres."

Tom Scott

LEO DIEGEL

"On his brilliant days he would have beaten any player in the world—a truly great golfer."

Al Watrous

"Diegel's greatest misfortune was that Walter Hagen just happened to be playing golf at the same time as he was."

Peter Alliss, 1988

HORTON SMITH

"I can truly say that I have played a lot of golf with Smith and have never once seen him putt badly."

Robert T. Jones, Jr.

Norman von Nida

"O.K., son, then you and I are a pair, because I'm the best golfer in Brisbane."

> **Walter Hagen,** responding to a small and young caddie who told Hagen, "I am the best caddie in Brisbane," 1929 (von Nida went on to great success as a professional.)

Byron Nelson

"At his peak Byron erred so infrequently that it could be boring to watch him."

> **Herbert Warren Wind**

"There is little doubt about the magnitude of Byron Nelson's achievements."

> **Peter Alliss, 1988**

"Nelson was one of the great champions and it was tragic that he found it necessary to retire when his game was at its zenith."

> **Will Grimsley, 1966**

"I was impressed by his simple style, which was theoretically perfect and completely orthodox."

> **Norman von Nida, 1956**

"Nelson the golfer will not be recalled as a player with the grace of a Vardon, a Jones, a Snead. He was quite simply efficient, an eliminator of errors once he had established his action, perhaps almost verging on the bland."

Peter Alliss

"At my best, I never came close to the golf that Nelson shoots."

Robert T. Jones, Jr.

"Byron was probably the greatest striker of the ball."

Tom Watson

"No man could hit a golf ball straighter than could Byron Nelson."

Ken Venturi, 1978

"He was, most likely, the best player in the late-Depression/pre-war era."

Pat Seelig, 1989

"WILD BILL" MEHLHORN

"I played with him at Shawnee-on-Delaware one time. He had about a three-foot putt. It was downhill. He putted the ball and played the next shot out of a bunker."

Ben Hogan

JIMMY DEMARET

"I regard him as the greatest sand player I have ever seen."

Dai Rees

"If Jimmy had concentrated on golf as much as laughing, he might have won more but I wouldn't have liked him."

Ben Hogan

SAM SNEAD

"It was a sad and unjust omission in such a distinguished career that he never won the American Open."

Michael McDonnell, 1982

"Sam Snead is to golf what Paul Bunyan is to the North Woods, John Henry to railroading and Black Bart to highwaymen—bigger than life."

Jim Murray

"He'd do whatever he had to do to get the ball in the hole. He didn't care how it looked."

Cary Middlecoff

"To Sam, hitting a golf ball is like a duck taking to water."

Norman von Nida, 1956

"No one could ever call Sam Snead the most gracious man in the world, but with the straw hat, the athletic walk, the arrogant stride and the broad hillbilly accent he is an exceptional person, and a helluva golfer."

Peter Alliss, 1981

"He has about the finest golf swing I've ever seen. But he is not a good general on the course."

Gene Sarazen

"There can never have been, in all the history of ball games, a player whose method of striking more exactly expressed perfection of style, power and beauty."

Pat Ward-Thomas

"Had Snead become United States Open champion, undoubtedly he would have been rated as the greatest American professional of all time."

Tom Scott

"There is no denying that there has never been a golfer with a more beautiful swing than Samuel Jackson Snead."

Peter Alliss

BEN HOGAN

"Not only does Hogan know more about hitting the golf ball than Palmer, but he knows more about it than Palmer and the other four top players in the world."

Tommy Bolt

S N E A D

"No one has ever hit a golf ball quite as he has. The sound of club against ball and turf was strangely different. There is no adequate descriptive word or nonword for it. It wasn't a thwock or clack or zunk. It was . . . different."

Al Barkow, 1980

"I believe that in the history of golf there has never been a man who could consistently hit the ball closer to the hole than Ben Hogan."

Jimmy Demaret, 1978

"Others were Jack, Billy, Arnie or Sam, but Hogan was Mr. Hogan to all save those who knew him well, and the title is more meaningful in America than Britain."

Pat Ward-Thomas, 1966

"The three things I fear most in golf are lightning, Ben Hogan and a downhill putt."

Sam Snead

"He may well have been the golfer of all ages."

Charles Price, 1978

"Probably the coldest and most rational champion golfer who ever lived."

Peter Alliss, 1981

"His determination and character obviously showed in his play but more in the manner he conquered himself, perhaps the hardest but most important task of every champion."

Michael McDonnell

"Ben Hogan is a golfing legend. No other word can suitably describe the greatest golfer of the immediate postwar years."

Peter Alliss, 1988

"If you have seen so much of golf and golfers, you can hardly fail to be intrigued by a man who plays it rather better than does anyone else in the world."

Henry Longhurst

"There are two things in life which Ben Hogan especially dislikes. One is losing a golf match. The other is teaching golf."

Jimmy Demaret, 1954

"His legs weren't strong enough to carry his heart around."

Grantland Rice, following the playoff in 1950 Los Angeles Open won by Snead. It was Hogan's first start after his near-fatal accident.

"Ben Hogan is the most merciless player of all the modern golfers."

Gene Sarazen, 1950

"He's the only player I have ever known to get an ovation from the fans on the practice tee. I've seen him playing practice rounds before a tournament and half his gallery was made up of other professionals."

Tommy Bolt

"He reached an awareness and understanding of the golf swing that went beyond mechanics and, with his interminable drill on the practice ground, he acquired an exhaustive self-knowledge."

Michael McDonnell

"To my mind, Ben Hogan is the greatest golfer that ever lived."

Jimmy Demaret, 1954

"The man who thought the game could be played like a machine, tried to play like a machine, and damned near did."

Charles Price, 1980

"I would like to be known as a gentleman first, and next as a golfer. That's all."

Ben Hogan, responding to
how he would like to be
remembered, 1987

"One thing is certain, Ben Hogan never had a natural swing."

Jimmy Demaret, 1978

"There has never been a finer golfer."

Peter Alliss

"Mr. Hogan, would you please sign my visor?"

> **Peter Jacobsen** at the
> Colonial National Invitational,
> 1990

"The paradox of Hogan was that his fame was an unwelcome price of his success."

> **Michael McDonnell**, 1982

"Hogan was elegant and magical to watch."

> **Peter Thomson**

"No other golfer has ever dedicated himself so unanimously to golf."

> **Herbert Warren Wind**

"If he had needed a 64 on his final round, you were quite certain he could have played a 64. Hogan gave you the distinct impression that he was capable of getting whatever score was needed to win."

> **Bernard Darwin** after Hogan
> shot a final round 68 to win
> the British Open, 1953

"Well, Ben, you've started a new trend. We're all going out tonight and try to get hit by a bus."

> **Tommy Bolt** following
> Hogan's victory in the
> U.S. Open at Oakland Hills,
> 1951

"I promise you Hogan knows more about striking a golf ball than any man who has ever lived."

Gary Player

"Hogan is a great player because he is able to make the right decision at the moment it must be made."

Walter Hagen

"There is little doubt that he has been the most accurate golfer, and probably the most formidable competitor that ever lived."

Pat Ward-Thomas

"Hogan is certainly the top thinker—shot by shot. He rarely guesses wrong or makes the slightest mistake. One reason is that he rarely has to guess. He knows."

Grantland Rice

"He concentrates better than anyone I ever saw."

Craig Wood

"Hogan is the greatest of all contemporary golfers and is on equal terms with Jones, Hagen and the bygone greats."

Norman von Nida, 1956

"When Hogan showed up."

Jimmy Demaret, when asked what was the turning point of his match in the 1946 PGA Championship which Hogan won by 10 and 9

"I thought I was a hard fighter. I thought Hagen and Sarazen were. We're not in a class with this fellow, Hogan. When he has a 90-yard shot to play, he expects to hole it."

Robert T. Jones, Jr.

LLOYD MANGRUM

"He was one of the most nerveless putters golf has known."

Charles Price, 1990

TOMMY BOLT

"Tommy Bolt was more than a golfer, he was an artist, perhaps the greatest shotmaker of all time."

Ken Venturi, 1978

"If we could have just screwed another head on his shoulders, he would have been the greatest golfer who ever lived."

Ben Hogan

"When we start ticking off the five or 10 greatest players of all time, his name comes up an awful lot."

Ed Sneed

"Tommy threw clubs with class."

Don January

"To me, his golf swing was perfect."

Tom Weiskopf

CARY MIDDLECOFF

"He has everything except bunker play. And, believe me, he could really putt."

                                                                    Dave Marr

"A slow, often frustratingly slow, player, he used to take a long time adjusting himself for each shot, but his actions were justified by the results."

                                                               Peter Alliss, 1988

BOBBY LOCKE

"I cannot imagine that there ever was a putter quite the equal of Locke, on all conditions of green, all over the world."

                                                               Pat Ward-Thomas

"Bobby was the prime example of someone who could not hit the ball, but really could play golf."

                                                                Henry Cotton

"Locke was perhaps the greatest putter ever seen outside the United States."

                                                                Peter Ryde, 1973

"It was Locke's putting that enabled him to take America by storm. He was the greatest—many still believe the greatest ever."

                                                                 Ken Bowden

Locke

Norman

Ballesteros

Thomson

GREATS

"No golfer was ever better balanced than Locke, no man was a more deadly judge of distance from 100 yards in, and surely no-one was ever a better putter."

Peter Alliss, 1981

"I believe he was the best judge of distance in the game."

Henry Longhurst

"The skill with which he handled his putter placed him in the same league as the greats—Walter Hagen and Bobby Jones—as a master of putting."

Peter Alliss, 1988

PETER THOMSON

"Thomson stood alone as the small-ball master of wind and of the trick shots needed on links where the British Open has always been held."

Peter Ryde, 1973

"Thomson's golf was a masterpiece of clean, true, straight hitting, the product of a swing that in its enduring rhythm and balance has few peers in his time."

Pat Ward-Thomas, 1966

"Peter made the game look ridiculously simple. He hit the ball straight, from A to B."

Peter Alliss, 1981

IVAN GANTZ

"I had been on tour just a short time when I first laid eyes on Ivan. I was walking down one fairway and looked over into another and there was this fellow with blood pouring out of a big gash on his forehead. It was Gantz and he had gone and hit himself in the head with his putter."

Don January

"If he'd miss a tee shot, he would back off in the crowd and stomp hell out of his driver. Later I found that Ivan stomped with just the toe of his shoe, never the heel. I stomped with the heel."

Tommy Bolt

MILDRED "BABE" ZAHARIAS

"She made women's golf. She put the hit in the swing."

Patty Berg

"Winning where Babe won is something special. She was one of the greatest athletes in the world and won here the year I was born. I think that was a lucky charm."

Hollis Stacy, following
U.S. Women's Open victory at
Salem Country Club, 1984

"She has set the pattern by which a champion should act on the course and off it and in the future all women golfers must be judged as they measure up to the standard or fail to do so."

Al Laney, 1954

"I'd give up every medal to have a baby."

Babe Zaharias when learning
Peggy Kirk Bell was expecting

"There have never been any half measures about anything that Mrs. Zaharias has done; nor were there any half shots about her golf. Such force leaves no room for finesse."

Enid Wilson, 1952

ROBERTO DE VICENZO

"Roberto, play as good as you can. I'm betting on you to be low Mexican."

Jimmy Demaret

ED FURGOL

"Man, could he drive that golf ball. His drives left those tees like they were late for supper."

Tommy Bolt

ARNOLD PALMER

"To place a president of the United States in proper historical perspective might take several generations, but to evaluate the impact of Arnold Palmer on golf we need not wait. He has meant more to the game than anyone, ever, in virtually every conceivable way."

Nick Seitz

"Concentration. Determination. These are the things that make Palmer the great player he is. You get the impression that if he has got a 5-iron shot to hole he will hole it."

Brian Huggett

"He's exciting. I think everything Palmer does is electrifying, the way he jerks his head and walks quickly. He uses the crowd as a spur. They've come to watch him play and he'll show them some good stuff."

Peter Alliss

"Sportswriters are given to extravagances and it was only natural that they should call Palmer the greatest golfer in the world. I never did. A newspaperman called me and asked me point blank if Palmer was the greatest golfer ever to play in the Masters. I told him, 'Heavens, no,' and asked if he'd ever heard of such fellows as Ben Hogan, Sam Snead, Byron Nelson and even Jack Nicklaus."

Robert T. Jones, Jr.

"In my opinion, Palmer is better than Hogan or Sam Snead. He's better than any golfer who ever played."

Gary Player, 1966

"He's the most special person ever to play the game."

Don Ohlmeyer, creator of the
Skins Game

"Palmer has the game and the ability to go after anything. He has the physique, the temperament. He has good fighting spirit without being temperamental."

Horton Smith, 1960

"Perhaps more than any other golfer, Arnold Palmer has helped to popularize the sport and to promote and improve the image of the game."

Peter Alliss, 1988

"Where other players are aloof and hide their feelings under an impassive mask, Palmer is all too obviously human."

Peter Dobereiner, 1970

"I'll always feel privileged to call Arnold a friend, a champion among champions."

Ken Venturi

"The real secret of the Palmer phenomenon was that he had star quality—a charisma that strikes a chord with the public and sets one man apart from all the rest."

Michael McDonnell, 1982

"It is difficult to see anyone who can beat him in the next 10 years if he chooses to come."

Henry Longhurst after Palmer won the British Open, 1961

"Arnold was the complete extrovert in the sense that he was the world's sweetheart, open, friendly, amicable."

Peter Alliss, 1981

P A L M E R

"He possessed a natural charm. He had the wide shoulders and tapering waist of a football halfback. His roundish, strong face ran the gamut of emotions. When making one of his fabled charges, his countenance would take on a grim mask of concentration. This would change immediately to a beaming smile when a birdie dropped."

Will Grimsley, 1961

"He's the biggest crowd pleaser since the invention of the portable sanitary facilities."

Bob Hope

"Palmer usually walks to the first tee unlike any other pro. He doesn't walk onto it as much as climb into it, almost as though it was a prize ring."

Will Grimsley

"He's most dangerous when he's on the ropes, ready to be counted out."

Gene Sarazen

"He had box-office appeal and, through him, golf prospered."

Michael McDonnell

"If your life depended on a putt, Palmer is the man to call."

Bob Rosburg

"Just the most exciting golfer the game has known since Walter Hagen."

Peter Alliss

"In historical terms, Arnold Palmer ranks with Harry Vardon and Walter Hagen as a major figure in the development of the sport."

Michael McDonnell, 1982

BILLY CASPER

"If you couldn't putt you'd be selling hot dogs on the 10th tee."

Ben Hogan after a
round with Casper in
Palm Beach Round Robin,
1957

"Billy Casper has won titles at more weight levels than Sugar Ray Leonard."

John Brodie

GENE LITTLER

"One of the greatest talents I've ever seen."

Ken Venturi

TONY LEMA

"Tony gave golf what Palmer gave golf."

Gene Sarazen

"Champions will come and champions will go but Tony Lema will always have a place in the hearts of everyone who met him and in the minds of everyone who saw him play."

Tom Scott

DOUG SANDERS

"Doug Sanders must surely rank as the finest golfer never to have won a major."

Peter Alliss, 1988

GARY PLAYER

"In the entire context of world sport, there is a case for saying that Gary Player is not just an outstanding golf champion, but has been one of the world's outstanding athletes."

Peter Alliss

"Gary Player is a very intense little man and his golf swing reflects his personality."

Bob Toski, 1978

"It is a measure of Player's skill that many of his championships were won on the most demanding golf courses in the world."

Michael McDonnell, 1982

"Player is possibly the most accomplished sand player in the world—he has been known to aim at bunkers."

Nick Seitz, 1978

"In my time Player and Hogan are the most dedicated golfers I've ever seen, and I've seen a few."

Jimmy Demaret, 1975

P L A Y E R

"He's the only guy I know who can shoot 80 and say he hit the ball super."

David Graham, 1975

"The thing I admire so much about him is that he just never wastes a stroke, not once in a year. He plays each shot for everything it's worth."

Byron Nelson

"He has such outright tenacity, such blazing determination, such a total conviction that nothing is impossible for him that although there are times when you just cannot make sense of him, cannot follow his logic, cannot begin to agree with him, his enormous ability and the sheer achievement of the man override everything."

Peter Alliss, 1981

MICKEY WRIGHT

"Mickey Wright had the best swing."

Patty Berg

"She had set standards of achievement that have not been surpassed, the most lasting contribution any player can give to their game, especially when, as with Mickey Wright, it is gracefully borne."

Pat Ward-Thomas

"Mickey had the best swing of either tour."

JoAnne Carner

"She was the best ever, no question. Her swing was absolutely flawless."

Sandra Palmer, 1985

"Mickey was much better than Babe Zaharias. No comparison. Babe was stronger, and maybe a better athlete—she was so well coordinated—but Mickey had a better golf swing, hit the ball better, could play rings around the Babe."

Betsy Rawls, 1986

WIFFI SMITH

"She is physically strong and is blessed with an ideal not-to-worry temperament which will stand her in good stead in a line of life which has already broken the spirits of quite a number of women."

Henry Longhurst, 1957

"The most powerful striker we had ever seen since Mrs. Zaharias."

Pat Ward-Thomas, 1961

AL GEIBERGER

"Allen looks like the world's longest chimney sweep. He's around 7 feet tall and could use his wedding ring for a belt. A two iron that talks."

Jim Murray

JACK NICKLAUS

"He has suffered a career-long comparison to the giant whose game he never saw—Bobby Jones."

George Peper, 1980

"You know he's gonna beat you, he knows he's gonna beat you and he knows you know he's gonna beat you."

Leonard Thompson

"I've never seen anyone who looks forward to combat the way Jack does."

Tom Weiskopf, 1978

"Nicklaus has reached his peak. He has been playing competitive golf since he was 14. No man can go to the trough that many times without a lot being taken out of him. I don't think he will get any better."

Sam Snead, 1963

"Not as sullen and intent as Hogan, he is similar to the Texas Hawk in the manner that he studies a golf course and then methodically brings it to its knees."

Will Grimsley, 1976

"Jack has had his eyes on lofty goals from the very beginning."

Ray Floyd, 1978

"I happen to think Nicklaus is the greatest ever. I know Jack thinks he is."

Frank Beard, 1991

NICKLAUS

"He stands in the highest echelon of the game with Vardon, Jones and Hogan."

Peter Alliss

"He plays a game with which I am not familiar."

Robert T. Jones, Jr.,
watching him win the
Masters, 1965

"It is possible to beat Jack, but nobody is in his class."

Lee Trevino

"Jack's got to start thinking about when it is time to retire."

Ken Venturi, 1986, prior to
Nicklaus's sixth Masters title

"Dad, I loved seeing you play today. It was the thrill of my life. I mean that was awesome."

Jackie Nicklaus, after
caddying for his father in the
Masters, 1986

"I finally found that guy I used to know on the golf course. It was me."

Jack Nicklaus, to his wife
after the Masters, 1986

"Jack Nicklaus is so strong that he does not require a full swing and at the top of it the club never reaches the horizontal."

Pat Ward-Thomas

"I agree that Jack was the number one player on the regular tour. If you ask me, he's the greatest golfer of all time, but he needs to learn humility."

Dave Hill, 1990

"Any time Jack makes up his mind to play his game, it doesn't make any difference what any of us do."

Lee Trevino, 1976

"Jack tries to be friendly, but I just don't feel comfortable with him. I feel like we're on different levels, which, of course we are. Unlike Palmer or Casper, Jack's never been just another pro. From his first day on the tour, he's been in the superstar class."

Frank Beard

"Indeed, Nicklaus dwarfed all his contemporaries and likened himself at times to an old gunfighter from the Wild West who became the target of every young newcomer anxious to make a name. Not many of them lasted long."

Michael McDonnell, 1982

"It is all too easy to describe a sportsman or woman as the 'greatest'. But in describing Jack Nicklaus it is impossible to think of any other suitable word to convey his stature in the world of golf. He has been, and still is, one of the greatest golfers of all time."

Peter Alliss, 1988

LEE TREVINO

"Listening to this guy all the way around will drive you crazy. He'll talk when we play again, but we won't listen."

Hale Irwin

"Trevino really has fun playing, which so many of the others don't. He combines pleasure with concentration to give himself a wonderful command of the situation. He's completely uninhibited."

Joseph C. Dey, Jr., 1968

"Had Trevino been schooled and tutored like Jack Nicklaus when he was young, he might have been as great as Nicklaus."

Bob Toski, 1978

"Lee gets down to the ball, stays with the ball, goes through the ball fairer and squarer than almost anyone you care to mention."

Peter Alliss, 1981

"Laddie, you're stronger than a garlic milkshake."

Gary Player

"I think that's the first time in my life I've heard him shut up."

Jack Nicklaus, commenting on Trevino's reaction to scoring a hole-in-one to win $175,000 in the Skins Game, 1987

"Lee Trevino is a class act."

Mike Hill, 1990

"Forget the PGA tour. There's no money in it."

Titanic Thompson, giving
advice to Trevino, 1966

"I don't have to change the initials on the towels and sheets."

Lee Trevino, replying to a
reporter who asked why he had
married another woman named
Claudia, 1984

"I was low Mexican last week. Since Lee won all that money last year, he became Spanish. He's not a Mexican anymore."

Homero Blancas, 1970

"Right now there's not a person alive on any tour anywhere in the world who can hit the ball better than Lee Trevino. I'm talking about hitting it pure every time."

Frank Beard, 1991

"Trevino took the stuffiness out of golf and put the fun back into the game."

Michael McDonnell, 1982

ART WALL

"I understand you are a very good putter. I'll have to watch how you do it."

Robert T. Jones, Jr.

HALE IRWIN

"In Hale Irwin you have a brilliant shotmaker, a great stylist and a man with tremendous competitive spirit."

Peter Alliss, 1988

TOM WATSON

"Watson is not a comer, he has arrived."

Jack Nicklaus, 1975

"Watson's eyes give away the unrelenting determination behind his relaxed manner."

Nick Seitz, 1978

"He has no limitations because he finds his limitations and fixes them."

Steve Reid

"He's absolutely fearless on the greens."

Johnny Miller, 1980

"His love of the game is loaded with passion, which translates to a level of reverence like that which Bob Jones displayed so engagingly."

Sandy Tatum, Jr., past
president of the USGA

"A pensive Tom Sawyer who, while the other boys were whitewashing fences, has become, politely but firmly, the best golfer in the world today."

John Updike, 1980

"Tom Watson knows where he's going and that's straight ahead."

Jack Nicklaus

"The only thing that can go wrong with his action is tempo, and his only visible fault is that he can get a shade too quick betimes."

Peter Alliss, 1981

"As aggressive as he is, he also plays an intelligent game."

Curtis Strange, 1991

JOANNE CARNER

"Big Mama is a lot like the Babe. She loves people and people love her."

Patty Berg, 1989

"I always thought JoAnne Carner was going to be the greatest amateur. She would have, if she had stayed an amateur."

Glenna Collett Vare, 1975

BEN CRENSHAW

"He's definitely the best putter I've ever seen."

> Curtis Strange, 1990

"Ben deserved it. He's been in the hunt in a lot of major championships. This is his first and I know what it must mean to him."

> Tom Watson, after finishing
> second to Crenshaw in the
> Masters, 1984

"The pressure on Ben was to prove he was another legend. I don't know if God could live up to the hope that accompanied Ben when he went on tour."

> Tom Kite, 1985

"Ben Crenshaw hits a fairway only every other eclipse of the moon. But he's won 14 tournaments."

> Jim Murray, 1989

"He hits into the woods so often he should get an orange hunting jacket."

> Tom Weiskopf, 1973

NANCY LOPEZ

"She has beautiful tempo, a beautiful putting stroke. She's a very fine player."

> Patty Berg, 1989

"Nancy Lopez was the female golfer of the decade—by a lot."

Frank Hannigan, 1989

"Nancy Lopez took the game to a higher level."

Jeff Williams, 1979

"Nancy never went through the same initiation as the rest of the LPGA women. She came out on Tour and simply shot her way right into the lead. But it wasn't beginner's luck."

JoAnne Carner, 1978

SEVE BALLESTEROS

"He's the best young golfer in the game."

Gary Player, 1980

"Severiano Ballesteros is the wonder of the age."

Peter Alliss, 1981

"Not since Arnold Palmer has golf seen skill, luck and courage blended so favorably in a rising young star."

Michael McDonnell, 1978

"Seve's never in trouble. We see him in trees quite a lot, but that looks normal to him."

Ben Crenshaw

"In terms of people I've seen in my lifetime, Ballesteros is as gifted as any."

John Jacobs, 1980

"He is a dummy, an idiot and a prima donna."

Juan Martija, mayor of Seve's
home town, Santander

"Nothing Seve does surprises anybody."

Gordon Brand,
when Seve passed up the
World Series of Golf, 1985

"Seve hits shots other people never think of."

Ben Crenshaw

"Seve hits the ball sideways too often to be considered a truly great player."

Tom Watson, 1980

"He's the best to come along since Nicklaus."

Tony Jacklin, 1980

"Charismatic. But so is a bull fighter."

Jim Murray, 1978

"Seve is as intelligent as anybody I've ever seen on a golf course."

Tony Jacklin

ANDY NORTH

"This game's all about winning when you have a chance to win. Andy does that."

> Johnny Miller, on the much
> maligned two-time U.S. Open
> champion

GREG NORMAN

"He overpowered the course when he needed to and he finessed it when he needed to. He's a very good player and getting better."

> Jack Nicklaus, 1984

"He's the longest, straightest driver we have. I think he can win anywhere."

> Curtis Strange, 1990

"I have always enjoyed Greg's attitude towards the game and his desire to win and be the best."

> Jack Nicklaus, 1988

FRED COUPLES

"He has no idea how strong he is. In Houston last year, I saw him hit a two iron 290 yards out of the rough. I just drooled when I saw it."

> Lee Trevino, 1985

MARK CALCAVECCHIA

"He tries to drag the course home to the cave by the hair."
                                                    Jim Murray

LARRY MIZE

"He has the potential to be a superstar. He reminds me a lot of Tom Watson years ago."
                                    Lee Trevino, two years before
                                    Mize won the 1987 Masters

BETH DANIEL

"In three years, she's going to be the best player out here."
                                            Mickey Wright, 1980

"She hits the ball higher and carries it farther than anyone else. I think she's the best player out here."
                                            Betsy King, 1990

CURTIS STRANGE

"If my tempo or balance begins to go awry, I'll watch Curtis Strange because he has exquisite balance throughout the swing."
                                            Peter Jacobsen

"He's got the guts of Tom Watson, but he's not as nice. Which is kind of nice."
                                        Thomas Boswell, 1989

PHIL MICKELSON

"The brightest young star we've seen come on the scene in a long, long time."

Jack Nicklaus, 1991

———————

DWIGHT D. EISENHOWER

"Almost immediately after becoming President, it became apparent that he intended making golf his chief form of recreation and that he would not be satisfied with a duffer's game."

Fred Byrod, 1975

"No one got as much pleasure as he did out of a fine shot or breaking 90."

Bob Hope, 1980

LAWRENCE TAYLOR

"He hits a golf ball harder than he hits a quarterback."

Billy Casper, after being paired with the Giants' linebacker in the Doral-Ryder Pro-Am, 1987

HOWARD HUGHES

"I never saw a fellow work harder. In a few months he was down in the 70s and collecting all he had lost . . . and more. They couldn't believe anyone could pick up the game in such short notice."

Willie Hunter,
Riviera Country Club
professional

WILLIAM HOWARD TAFT

"Taft, so far as we know, was the earliest president to play the Royal and Ancient game, and if you believe Walter J. Travis, winner of the national amateur in 1900, 1901 and 1903, William Howard was a pretty fair swinger."

Robert Cromie

GERALD R. FORD

"He's a powerful golfer who can hit the ball 250 yards—in any direction."

Bob Hope, 1980

"He is capable of being a very good player. If he had the time to practice, he could be a good solid six or seven handicapper."

Jack Nicklaus, 1975

JACKIE GLEASON

"Gleason's the only golfer I know with a spigot on his 5-iron."

Bob Hope, 1985

BOB HOPE

"Bob's got a great short game. Unfortunately it's off the tee."
Jimmy Demaret

"In spite of all the wonderful gifts and mementos given me, if I could have one special piece of memorabilia, it would be the first dollar Bob Hope ever paid on a bet lost on a golf course. The search for the bill wouldn't be difficult. It's still in Bob's right-hand pants pocket."
Gerald R. Ford

"Nobody takes his golf as seriously as Hope, and he would rather win a golf match than an Oscar."
Bing Crosby, 1953

ALAN SHEPARD AND THE MOON SHOT

"Because of the cumbersome suit I was wearing, I couldn't make a very good pivot on the swing, and I had to hit the ball with just one hand. It would normally have gone about 30 yards. Up there it went 200. My second shot was a shank. It went 40 or 50 yards. A ball won't hook or slice on the Moon because it has no atmosphere, so this was a pure shank."
Alan Shepard

"Here's the man who won the Lunar Open, and his closest competitor was 250,000 miles away."
Gene Cernan

PAR 3
1500 yds

F O R E !

PHIL HARRIS

"Phil is the only man I know who keeps his left arm straight all day, and bent all night."

Paul Hahn

MICHAEL JORDAN

"Jordan is about as close to making the Tour as Ian Woosnam is to dunking a basketball. Jordan's handicap is around a seven. Tour players are around a plus seven on the toughest courses in the world. Head-to-head, Woosnam only beats Jordan by about 14 strokes. To say that Jordan could learn in the offseason what Woosnam has spent 12 hours a day perfecting since he was a kid is a flat-out insult."

Rick Reilly, 1991

4

Humor

There's an old story about an American golfer who made his first trip to Scotland. No different than golfers anywhere, he wanted to play where it all began—the Old Course. The great day arrived and with a caddie at his side, he waited to hit his drive from the first tee. The caddies at St. Andrews can be intimidating. Most are seasoned veterans expecting reasonable golf from their players.

The American proceeded to top his tee shot, slice the second and hit the third into the burn. He turned to his caddie and said, "Golf's a funny game." The unsmiling caddie replied, "Aye, but it was nae meant to be."

Perhaps the reason there is so much humor in golf is because it is such a serious game. We don't mean to do funny things when we play, they just happen.

———

"Golf is not a funeral though both can be very sad affairs."

Bernard Darwin

"Golf is based on honesty. Where else would someone admit to a 7 on an easy par 3?"

Jimmy Demaret

"It doesn't much matter what kind of a clubhead is on one end of that shiny metal shaft if a fat head is on the other."

Robinson Murray, 1951

"Walter Hagen is known as the first man to make a million dollars in golf, and spend it. Sam Snead was the first to make a million—and save two million."

Fred Corcoran, 1965

"One thing about Walter, he wouldn't spend your money any faster than he spends his own."

Bob Harlow, Hagen's manager

"You can't alibi a 100 score down to 80."

Don Herold, 1952

"It is good sportsmanship to not pick up lost golf balls while they are still rolling."

Mark Twain

"The first 18 holes give a golf club its reason to exist; the 19th gives it the money."

Robinson Murray, 1951

"If your wife interferes with your golf, get a new wife. If your business interferes with your golf, get a new business."

Don Herold, 1952

"The average caddie can find five balls while looking for yours—which he can't find."

Robinson Murray, 1951

"It is a law of nature that everybody plays a hole badly when playing through."

Bernard Darwin

"The two easiest shots in golf are the fourth putt and the explosion shot off the tee."

Ring Lardner

"I think that good-looking form is one of the secrets of good golf. Look beautiful and you'll play beautiful. However, some old codgers with whom I play, play mighty ugly and beat the pants off of me."

Don Herold, 1952

"If you think it's hard to meet people, try picking up the wrong golf ball."

Jack Lemmon

"Golf should never be talked about in a sitting position. The lecturer, in order to gain maximum effectiveness, should act out his stories."

Stephen Baker, 1962

"People who wear white shoes are either golfers or tourists."

Jimmy Cannon

"The tearing up of a card is generally regarded as a rather discreditable business, showing at once vanity and pusillanimity in the tearer; and I must say that I do feel something more of a man when I have gone on to the bitter end and handed in the horrid thing."

Bernard Darwin, 1932

"Golf actually makes for international understanding, drawing men together as it does through their common sorrows. The standard alibis have been freely translated into every known language, including bad language."

Robinson Murray, 1951

"There have been days when all I got out of golf was the oxygen."

Don Herold, 1952

"Nicklaus, you play so slow that when I started out I was clean-shaven."

Foster Brooks

"Lady, I'm the U.S. Open champion. What do you expect, ground balls?"

Lee Trevino, to a woman
expressing awe at Trevino's
practice shots, 1969

"Experts who have studied the matter assure us that the mind can only think of one thing at a time. Obviously they have never made a study of golfers, or they would lower their estimate."

Robinson Murray, 1951

"Golf is not a particularly natural game. Like sword-swallowing, it has to be learned."

Brian Swarbrick, 1973

"Contrary to what many amateurs have been led to believe, the golf ball is not a natural enemy of mankind."

Arnold Palmer, 1963

"You must never forget that golf is supposed to be a game of relaxation. It should take your mind off your work, your mortgage, your income tax, and introduce fresh and much more serious problems into your life."

Stephen Baker, 1962

"A game whose aim is to hit a very small ball into an even smaller hole, with weapons singularly ill-suited for the purpose."

Winston Churchill

"Golf is a good walk spoiled."

Mark Twain

"Golf is great exercise, particularly climbing in and out of the carts."

Jack Berry, golf writer for
The Detroit News, 1991

"Golf is a four-letter word. And it's probably caused as much passion, delight and anguish as some of the more notorious four-letter words."

Peter Alliss, 1982

"Playing with your spouse on the golf course runs almost as great a marital risk as getting caught playing with someone else's anywhere else."

Peter Andrews, 1987

"Walter Hagen used to say a bad shot never troubled him because he always figured to hit about so many of them every round. Maybe if he had hit 30 or 40 of them like some of us it might have shaken him up a little."

Robinson Murray, 1951

"The hardest shot is a mashie at 90 yards from the green, where the ball has to be played against an oak tree, bounces back into a sandtrap, hits a stone, bounces on the green and then rolls into the cup. That shot is so difficult I have made it only once."

Zeppo Marx

5

Golf Courses

In all sports, the most overworked term to describe an action or a player seems to be "great" and that is particularly true about golf courses. For many years, attempts have been made to select the best courses in the world, the United States or just about any geographical location consisting of at least two courses. Part of the problem in making those selections is that few of the panel expressing their views have played on all the layouts. The lists create a good deal of disagreement when they are published. Jimmy Demaret, one of the panel members a number of years ago for *Golf Digest,* did not include Oakland Hills in his top 10. That was a blow to the members as they had previously been in that lofty position and even named the flights in their annual member-guest tournament after the top 10 courses in the country.

Angry letters followed. The head professional at Oakland Hills at the time said the only reason Demaret voted against the club was because he shot 76 the last time he played it. Others said it was the direct result of the club not hosting USGA events, having changed to being the host for the PGA Championship instead. They went on to say the panel was dominated by USGA-types, whatever that meant.

In my opinion, one of the reasons a golf course is considered great, or even good, is the exposure it receives. If a course serves as the venue for a tournament or championship, people get to see it. More importantly those who serve on selection committees have the opportunity to see, or play it. An example may be in the Liverpool area where both Royal Liverpool (Hoylake) and Royal Lytham & St. Annes receive a great deal of attention. But the area is also blessed with another course of high quality—Formby. The problem is that Formby is rarely played in competition, hosting the British Amateur only once every 10 years or so.

Another is Maidstone on Long Island. It is said by many to be the equal of Shinnecock Hills, but only members and the few lucky people who are invited as guests know about the wonderful layout. A notable exception is Pine Valley. It has only hosted one event of major importance and that was the Walker Cup. Still, its reputation makes it a regular on any list of the 10 best courses in the United States or the world, if not the number one ranking.

Certainly Augusta National deserves its plaudits, but if it was not the site of The Masters, few would know of its beauty and challenging greens. Of course, it is also possible that much of what has been done to Augusta National over the years would not have been done if the course did not host such an important tournament.

Tradition plays an important role in the recognition of a golf course. Merion, for example, will always be known as the site of Jones's final victory when he won the Grand Slam and where he also made his debut on the national scene as a lad of 14 in the U.S. Amateur. When Palmer drove the first green in the final round of the 1960 U.S. Open, putting the word "charge" into golf, he helped to make the reputation of Cherry Hills. Hogan's victories in the Los Angeles and U.S. Opens in 1948 were both at Riviera, which Jimmy Demaret dubbed "Hogan's Alley," giving it everlasting fame. Oakland Hills didn't suffer when Hogan said he was happy he brought the "Monster" to its knees following his closing 67 in the 1951 U.S. Open. He felt it was his finest competitive round and members still hold an annual event with the same pin positions and tee markers used during that round.

To the best of my knowledge, that was the first time a course was referred to as a "Monster." Then it was used again by Frank Strafaci. He was describing the 18th hole at Doral's Blue Course. The name not only stuck, but was expanded to include the entire course and now it is called the Blue Monster. To take it a step further, a new course was built near Panama City, Florida. Even before it opened, the developer named it The Monster. Ben Hogan probably didn't know what he was starting in 1951.

Many of the famous sites have more than one course. St. Andrews has four—the Old, New, Eden and Jubilee. When most people talk about St. Andrews, they are actually referring to the Old Course. When Merion is mentioned, they mean the East Course, just as it's the West at Winged Foot, #3 at Medinah, the South Course at Oakland Hills, #2 at Pinehurst and the Ailsa at Turnberry.

Not everyone has the same feelings about a course. Jones disliked the Old Course after his first visit although it later became his favorite. Sam Snead made some derogatory remarks about St. Andrews and to this day is not enamoured by it. Augusta National normally draws raves, except from Lee Trevino who claimed the course was designed for those who hooked the ball and that a golfer who hit a fade, like Trevino, couldn't win there. No one ever asked him how Jimmy Demaret was able to win three Masters and he not only faded the ball, but would hit a big slice on occasion.

One thing is certain, every course has its own personality. The most boring can still be far more interesting than a football field.

———

"I think it should be remembered that golf started by the sea; it was played on a type of country called 'links,' which is the link between the sea and the land, and today most of our great golf courses are links, but you cannot have links anywhere else but by the seaside."

Lord Brabazon of Tara,
1952

"The grounds on which golf is played are called links being the barren, sandy soil from which the sea has retired in recent geological times. In their natural state links are covered with long, rank, benty grass and gorse . . . links are too barren for cultivation; but sheep, rabbits, geese and professionals pick up a precarious livelihood on them."

Sir W. G. Simpson, 1892

"Originally there were only nine holes at St. Andrews: The golfer then turned round and played over much the same ground home again but using different greens. Hence the total of 18 holes for a golf links is of quite an accidental origin."

Charles Mortimer, 1952

"What makes a golf course beautiful is its setting."

Charles Price, 1978

"A golf course is something as mysterious as St. Andrews, as majestic as Pine Valley, as ferocious as Oakmont, as subtle as Hoylake, as commonplace as Happy Knoll."

Charles Price, 1962

"No two courses are the same, even though they be similar in character."

John L. Low, 1903

"I discovered to my enjoyable relief that a great golf course, like a supreme piece of music, does not reveal its splendors at a first or second reading; nor for most of us, ever."

Alistair Cooke

"The first purpose of any golf course should be to give pleasure."

Robert T. Jones, Jr.

"No golfer has ever been forced to say to himself with tears, 'There are no more links to conquer.'"

John L. Low, 1903

COURSES

"There's some merit in the suggestion that all golf courses should be 19 holes—with the first not counting."

Don Herold, 1952

"And how beautiful the vacated links at dawn, when the dew gleams untrodden beneath the pendant flags and the long shadows lie quiet on the green; when no caddie intrudes upon the still and silent lawns, and you stroll from hole to hole and drink in the beauties of a land to which you know you will be all too blind when the sun mounts high and you toss for the honor."

Arnold Haultain, 1908

GOLF COURSE ARCHITECTURE

"On a truly great course the challenge is both real and vigorously stated, the shot values unmistakably of a high order, and the design qualities uncommon."

Jim Finnegan, 1976

"One of the basic principles of the first architects seemed to be a desire for as many blind shots as possible."

Pat Ward-Thomas, 1966

"I think that I always will adhere to my old theory that a controlled shot to a closely guarded green is the surest test of any man's golf."

A. W. Tillinghast, who built
Winged Foot and several other
outstanding courses

"I try to build courses that will challenge the golfer of tomorrow, not the golfer of today."

                                        Jack Nicklaus, 1990

"The way things are now, women are afterthoughts with most course designers."

                                        Amy Alcott, 1990

"The difference between the golf courses of America and of Great Britain can best be expressed by the two words 'artificial' and 'natural': and that means a whole lot more than the mere presence or absence of the fabrication of man."

                                        Robert T. Jones, Jr., 1926

"What an institution it is, the clubhouse, and the bar. I often think that the golf club bar is built before the course and is really the key factor in the club."

                                        Peter Alliss, 1981

"'Championship course' is a catch-penny label used by resort developers and signifies only that the course in question is a dreary slog of over 7,000 yards for anyone foolish enough to play it off the back tees."

                                        Peter Dobereiner, 1978

"Every hole should be a hard par and an easy bogey."

                                        Robert Trent Jones

"The chief object of every golf architect or greenkeeper worth his salt is to imitate the beauties of nature so closely as to make his work indistinguishable from nature itself."

> **Alister Mackenzie,** who designed Cypress Point and Augusta National among others

"Just because a course is 7,000 yards long, it's not great."

> **Frank Hannigan**

"The old-style courses were designed to make a player hit a variety of shots—high, low, draw, fade, bump and run, floating chips. Now with a lot of the new courses, our only choice is to hit high and soft."

> **Corey Pavin**

"If some hole does not possess striking individuality through some gift of nature, it must be given as much as possible artificially, and the artifice must be introduced in so subtle a manner as to make it seem natural."

> **A. W. Tillinghast**

"Saw a course you'd really like, Trent. On the first tee, you drop the ball over your shoulder."

> **Jimmy Demaret** to Robert Trent Jones after his alteration of the Donald Ross-designed Oakland Hills for the U.S. Open, 1951

"We've built some long courses, too long, really, for anybody but a pro. That's for the members' egos, because they like to brag about the length of their course."

Joe Lee, 1985

"We can build the greatest courses in the world, but if they are not properly maintained, they are nothing."

Robert Trent Jones

"The best course architecture is an imitation of nature."

Tommy Armour, 1959

"The best architects feel it to be their duty to make the path to the hole as free as possible from annoying difficulties for the less skillful golfers, while at the same time presenting to the scratch players a route calling for the best shots at their command."

Robert Hunter, 1926

"The best way to build a golf course is to start 200 years ago."

Peter Dobereiner, 1982

THE GAME'S GREATEST COURSES

ATLANTA ATHLETIC CLUB

"It's not a great course, but it could become great with some more changes."

P. J. Boatwright, prior to the club hosting the U.S. Open, 1976

"Those par four holes are so long that when you get to a 410-yarder you feel it's like a gimme."

Johnny Miller, 1976

AUGUSTA NATIONAL

"Augusta is as good as any. There's no rough."

Ben Hogan

"I know of no other course where the greens have so much contour."

Byron Nelson, 1966

"We got Dr. Mackenzie to lay out the course, but in my book, Bob Jones was the real architect. He is just too modest to admit the part he played."

Jerry Franklin, an original
member of the club

"Augusta National looks easy. It can be easy and it can be hard as hell, but it's always pleasant."

Norman von Nida, 1956

"It reminds me of the course I grew up on, Pedrena in Santander, Spain, only better. When I think of Augusta, I think of green. It's as beautiful as a postcard."

Seve Ballesteros

"The fairways are wide at Augusta and there isn't much danger of getting into the rough; you don't have to be much of a golfer to stay in the fairways."

Arnold Palmer

"You've got to really hit it big at Augusta. The longer you hit it, the more lofted clubs you can use for your approach. It's a very aggressive guy's course off the tee."

Greg Norman, 1990

"Augusta is the only course where they trick up the fringes."

Greg Norman, 1991

"Augusta is not a difficult course for the weekend amateur who is frankly looking for bogeys. But for the player who is out for pars and birdies, it can be a real tough course."

Robert T. Jones, Jr.

"This is a humbling course."

Gary Player

"It is such a tough course with the fast, sloping greens. On any other course, if you get a little nervous with your approach shot and put it 20 feet on the wrong side of the hole, it doesn't matter so much. But at Augusta, that's an automatic three-putt."

Nick Faldo, 1990

BALLYBUNION

"Very simply, Ballybunion revealed itself to be nothing less than the finest seaside course I have ever seen."

Herbert Warren Wind

BALTUSROL

"Baltusrol has one of the world's truly great courses among a huge number of courses that are called great, but actually aren't even very good."

Charles Price, 1980

BANFF SPRINGS

"Surley the most spectacular course in the world."

Peter Dobereiner, 1978

"If ever a course qualified for greatness on the grounds of beauty and dramatic setting alone, it would be Banff Springs."

Bob Ferrier, 1990

BUTLER NATIONAL

"Excluding the U.S. Open sites, Butler is the toughest course we play."

Tom Kite

CARNOUSTIE

"There are really 365 Carnousties, different golf courses with the varying weather each day of the year."

Peter Dobereiner, 1974

"Moody as Maria Callas, it rouses to fury when the westerlies come roaring out of the Atlantic across the width of Scotland."

Fred Tupper, 1975

"Carnoustie is one of the most rambling courses in the world, in addition to being one of the best."

Charles Price, 1980

"Quite possibly the most difficult in Scotland."

Robert Sommers, 1989

"A good swamp spoiled."

Gary Player

"Rarely can it be said of any course that it has no weakness, but this is true of Carnoustie."

Pat Ward-Thomas, 1976

"Carnoustie is simply an uninspiring course at first glance."

Steve Melnyk

"The last three holes at Carnoustie with the wind blowing from the east make up just about the most testing and perilous finish in all golf."

Bernard Darwin, 1931

"The rough is impossible. Impossible to stay out of. Impossible to play out of. But I guess I'd rather be in it 40 yards ahead of everybody else."

Jack Nicklaus, 1968

"It is still a great golf course that demands every shot in the bag."

Tony Jacklin, 1968

CHAMPIONS

"Whenever we played a course we looked for its best features, including its clubhouse and mode of operation. When the time came to build Champions, Jimmy [Demaret] and I were agreed on what we wanted to accomplish."

Jack Burke, Jr.

CONGRESSIONAL

"This is a long, difficult course and it plays a lot longer than its yardage. You hit so many shots uphill."

Jack Nicklaus

CROOKED STICK

"The course is so long I had to take the curvature of the Earth into consideration."

David Feherty, 1991

Cypress Point

"The course and the esthetics are delightful. Each hole is different. You can see each hole from the tee and each hole is totally different from the others."

William Campbell

"I would be happy to play Cypress Point the rest of my life."

Peter Alliss, 1981

"The real wonder of Cypress Point is how anybody can keep his mind on playing golf over it."

Pat Ward-Thomas, 1976

"It's fair. It's challenging. It's beautiful. It's natural. And, for the average player, its holes are within reach, lengthwise."

Joseph C. Dey, Jr.

"To play there is a privilege."

Bob Ferrier, 1990

"The best 17-hole golf course in the world."

Jimmy Demaret, showing his disdain for the 18th

"Majestic woodland, a hint of links and heathland here and there and the savage nobility of the coast made for unforgettable holes."

Pat Ward-Thomas

"The Sistine Chapel of golf."

Sandy Tatum, Jr.

"If ever a golf course could be said to have achieved perfection in combining scenery and golfing merit then this is it."

Peter Dobereiner, 1982

DORAL

"The truth is, the 18th is the best I've played, but the figures are there to show you the other holes aren't as tough."

Frank Strafaci, who
dubbed the 18th as the
"Blue Monster," a name
which spilled over to the
entire course

ESSEX

"It's one of the few courses I've played that you get a chance to use every club in the bag."

Johnny Miller, 1976

"Where have you been hiding this course the past 20 years?"

Arnold Palmer, 1976

FIRESTONE

"It's a boring course. You can fall asleep on it because you're always hitting the same kind of shots—woods or long irons."

Jack Nicklaus

FORMBY

"I do not say dogmatically that it is the best, but it is an old friend and wonderfully good and charming."

Bernard Darwin

"Formby, even if it is more unassuming than most, is second to none of them."

Bob Ferrier, 1990

HARBOUR TOWN LINKS

"I wished they hadn't asked, but when they asked about the conditions of the course I had to be frank and tell them that other than bumpy greens, spotty fairways and muddy tee boxes, it was okay."

Lee Trevino, 1989

HAZELTINE NATIONAL

"They ruined a good farm when they built this course."

Dave Hill, 1970

INDIANWOOD

"It looked like Scotland. Tall, reed-like foliage lined the fairways, turning them into deep green runways that seemed to get narrower each day. Some called it heather, like the authentic stuff in Scotland. Some called it fescue. Everybody who parachuted a tee shot into it called it trouble."

Gary Van Sickle, 1989

"Subtract its trees, and you might well have been walking the coasts of Scotland, England and Ireland—yet there were no coasts to speak of."

George Eberl, 1989

INVERNESS

"Inverness is kept in such magnificent condition, it is one of those rare courses where you could walk in any day of the week and play the U.S. Open."

Tom Fazio

"My ball was in the middle of one green and the name on my ball was touching the fringe."

Lee Trevino

LOS ANGELES

"It's as hard to get into as Windsor Castle, so exclusive you can get the bends just driving by it."

Jim Murray

MEDINAH #3

"It is a great, great golf course."

Curtis Strange, 1990

"Medinah is a nice course, but the greens are too roly-poly with too many humps. I just don't think its fair."

Dave Rummulls, 1989

"Its final three holes may be as demanding as any others in the golfing universe."

Joe Schwendeman, 1975

MERION

"The astonishing thing about Merion is that it is not at all overpowering in aspect."

Herbert Warren Wind

"Acre for acre it may be the best test of golf in the world."

Jack Nicklaus

"A lady member told me she doesn't know anything about the rough here because she's never been in it. I can only think she's never left the clubhouse."

George Archer

"Many of the modern architects could take a lesson by coming here and looking at the course."

Billy Casper

"This is the type of course where you feel after every round you play that you can break 70 the next round. You are sure of it. But somehow you don't. You are even surer the next time, but something always happens that you weren't looking for."

Walter Hagen

"Within moments of setting eyes on it I was reminded of England as by no other course in America."

Pat Ward-Thomas

"It is easily the best short championship course in the country and, regardless of length, one of the truly great ones."

Charles Price, 1980

"Merion may well be the classic course of American golf."

Robert Sommers, 1971

MUIRFIELD

"Muirfield is a traditional links and the fairest of them all, with hazards clearly visible and splendid views across the Firth of Forth."

Peter Dobereiner, 1978

"Muirfield is a patrician among golf courses."

Bob Ferrier, 1990

"No course in the British Isles embraces more of the qualities one seeks in a great and fair challenge of skill than Muirfield."

Pat Ward-Thomas, 1976

"It is on the flat side and at the first glance some people look upon it almost as an inland course, but after a round or two one becomes greatly impressed by the good golf that is to be obtained upon it and its excellent testing capacity."

Harry Vardon, 1905

"Muirfield is remarkably close-knit for so great a course. The original layout dates back to 1891, relatively new by Scottish standards, and it is as nearly perfect as a golf course design can get."

Charles Price, 1980

"This course is lying there waiting for you and if you snooze, you lose."

Doug Sanders

"The design is as fair as human ingenuity can devise, with only one blind shot on the course."

Peter Dobereiner, 1982

"I love this place. I love the feel of it, the smell of it, the taste of it. I love the turf, the feel of my spikes in it. I love the people."

Tom Watson, 1987

"Muirfield is a links, but it is not on the sea. The gently undulating dune land is about a mile inland."

Peter Dobereiner

"The fairest and best links course in Britain and Ireland."

Ben Wright, 1979

MUIRFIELD VILLAGE

"Muirfield Village is the first course to be planned right from the drawing board as a tournament site."

Peter Dobereiner, 1974

"I don't really think I enjoy the course. That is no reflection on the course. It is just such hard work."

Roger Maltbie

"They're (the greens) so slick that if you mark your ball, your dime better have spikes."

Lee Trevino, 1978

MUSSELBURGH

"I have always thought and still think that anyone who has learnt to play well on Musselburgh could give a good account of himself on any course in the world."

J. E. Laidlay

OAK HILL

"I'd hate to be a member here and play it the other 51 weeks."

Andy Bean, during the
PGA Championship, 1980

OAKLAND HILLS

"The Lord intended this for a golf course."

Donald Ross

"The course is playing the players instead of the players playing the course."

Walter Hagen, during the
U.S. Open, 1951

"This is the toughest par 70 I've ever seen."

Bernhard Langer, following a
practice round in 1975

"Oakland Hills was as much of a piece of cake as it will ever be and I didn't get to the icing."

Jack Nicklaus, after
shooting 294 in the
PGA Championship, 1979

"I honestly feel this is the hardest course in the world; I haven't played on them all, but this is the toughest I've ever seen."

Ben Hogan, 1951

"This is the greatest round of golf I've ever played."

Ben Hogan, after his closing
67 to win the U.S. Open,
1951

"You play a course like this and you want to beat it. Each hole has to be played differently. You play one hole one way with one type of shot and the next hole may play almost the opposite way. If offers a continuous challenge. I'm not a machine, only a golfer, and Oakland Hills was designed for some kind of super golfer that I've never seen yet. Yes, it was satisfying to bring the monster to its knees by going under par on the final round, but I don't know if I could ever do it again no matter how badly I needed it or how hard I tried."

Ben Hogan, 1951

"The monster bit back."

Dave Barr, after the final
round of the U.S. Open, 1985

OAKMONT

"They're the fastest greens I've ever seen."

Hubert Green

"Pittsburgh's old Oakmont, sitting on a plateau above the Allegheny River, with a desert of sand spread over 187 bunkers and with greens as slippery as marble stairs."

Fred Byrod, 1973

"This is a course where good putters worry about their second putts before they hit the first one."

Lew Worsham

"When you're eight feet away, you have to putt defensively. And it's tough to get close to the hole. It's tough to make birdies here."

Ben Crenshaw

"Oakmont has always had the reputation of cutting the greens even closer than the USGA prescribes for its Open."

John Ross, 1978

"These greens are so slick that nobody I know uses any kind of a putter except a blade. If you used a mallet-head—well that's like getting a back-rum with a sledge-hammer."

Lew Worsham

"If I don't get out of this trap pretty soon, my clothes are going to go out of style."

Bob Hope

OLD WARSON

"Old Warson has gotta be among the best jobs Jones ever did. Maybe the best."

Bob Goalby, 1971

OLYMPIC

"The longest short course in the world."

Ben Hogan

"If Olympic Club were human, it'd be Bela Lugosi. I think it turns into a bat at midnight."

Jim Murray

"It's a dynamite course. It makes you hit the shots. If you don't, it will kill you."

Tom Kite

"The course winds a subtle and attractive way through groves of cypress, pine and fir, and is a splendid, challenging test of golf."

Pat Ward-Thomas, 1966

"Playing holes three, four, five and six is like walking through a minefield."

Ben Crenshaw

"I think it's the best Open course I've ever seen. It's like a fairyland, one of those courses you just love to play."

Larry Nelson

"This is not a golf course, it's a paid political assassin, a king killer."

Jim Murray

PEBBLE BEACH

"Of all the grand strolls in golf, easily the most thrilling is along the eight heroic holes that border the Pacific at Pebble Beach."

Charles Price, 1980

"This is the worst set of U.S. Open greens I've ever putted on."

Billy Casper, 1972

"This is the finest strategy course in the world."

Jack Nicklaus

"The name Pebble Beach might suggest a seaside course in the manner of the links of Britain. But it is far from that. I can think of no approximate parallel."

Pat Ward-Thomas, 1966

PINE VALLEY

"Pine Valley is replete with classic golf holes, great in the sense that they would be magnificent holes even without its horrifying footprinted sandy wastes."

Robert Trent Jones

"The great golf course in the world."

Chick Evans, 1916

"Pine Valley is the perfect example of penal architecture, the ultimate test for the giants of golf."

Pat Ward-Thomas, 1976

"Pine Valley enjoys a reputation among golfers as a course that has 18 perfect holes, each one the best of its type and all blended together in intricate simplicity and perfect unison."

H. B. Martin, 1936

"Within its forest of pines, you cannot see more than one hole at a time, with the result that you get the eerie feeling that you and the rest of your foursome are playing the course by yourselves."

Charles Price, 1980

"No course presents more vividly and more severely the basic challenge of golf—the balance between fear and courage."

Pat Ward-Thomas, 1957

"An examination in golf."

Bernard Darwin

"Everyone who plays golf has heard of Pine Valley, few have had the luck to play there. I look on it as the greatest of all inland courses, the perfect 'examination' of the golfer's physical and psychological powers."

Henry Longhurst

"It's tough but fair. It's the kind of course that rewards a good shot but penalizes a poor one. It's a rugged course and that's exactly the way golf courses should be."

Arthur Brown, longtime president of Pine Valley

"We think that we shall never see
A tougher course than Pine Valley
Trees and traps wherever we go
And clumps of earth flying through the air
This course was made for you and me,
But only God can make a THREE."

Jack McLean and Charlie Yates, members of the British and American Walker Cup teams, after the 1936 matches

"It's beautiful and it's horrible. No, no—of course, those aren't the words, but you understand what I mean."

Jay Siegel

"Pine Valley is the shrine of American golf because so many golfers are buried there."

Ed Sullivan

"Pine Valley fills you with dread and delight . . . it takes your breath away . . . it's a monster, but it's beautiful."

Robert Trent Jones

"Suffering is supposed to be good for the soul and certainly a round at Pine Valley is a salutory experience for anyone foolish enough to believe that he has conquered the game of golf."

Peter Dobereiner, 1982

"There is a sense of privilege as well as rare experience in visiting Pine Valley, for it has no parallel anywhere."

Pat Ward-Thomas, 1957

"Pine Valley's not so tough if you can hit the ball straight, keep it out of the sand and putt reasonably well."

Arnold Palmer

PINEHURST

"There has never been a better example of the sow's-ear-to-silk-purse metamorphosis than the miracle that James Tuft and Donald Ross wrought in changing a worthless piece of sandy wasteland in North Carolina into Pinehurst."

Robert Trent Jones

"In the minds of many Americans, Pinehurst is synonymous with golf."

William Davis, founder of
Golf Digest

"The man who doesn't feel emotionally stirred when he golfs at Pinehurst beneath those clear blue skies and with the pine fragrance in his nostrils is the one who should be ruled out of golf for life."

Tommy Armour

PORTMARNOCK

"Portmarnock is possibly the finest expression of links golf to be found anywhere."

Peter Dobereiner, 1978

PRESTWICK

"It is an excellent test to apply to a would-be champion, although there have been complaints that this course is also short."

Harry Vardon, 1905

"Every feature that a golfer wants is here: great sandhills with little valleys beyond them, and the Pow Burn."

Peter Lawless

ROYAL LYTHAM & ST. ANNES

"A quite magnificent natural golf course of firm fairways, endless traps brimming with powdery sand, tenacious rough, humps and hollows and beautiful, velvety greens."

Mark McCormack

ROYAL ST. GEORGES

"This is as nearly my idea of heaven as is to be attained on any earthly links."

Bernard Darwin

"There is scarcely a hole at which a player who half hits his ball from the tee does not find himself in serious difficulties, demanding an unusually brilliant recovery and especially good play until he has holed out."

Harry Vardon, 1905

ROYAL TROON

"For me, all that is wonderful and challenging about links golf in Scotland is found at the Royal Troon Golf Club."

Tom Weiskopf

"Troon, abounding in sandhills, is very fair and the player needs to be very skillful to get 'round it in a low score."

Harry Vardon, 1905

St. Andrews

"I wish that every man who plays golf should play at St. Andrews once."

Gene Sarazen

"When you walk the Old Course, you know you are treading on hallowed ground. The only time I had a similar experience was when I first saw the battlefields of Gettysburg."

Charles Price, 1980

"Here is the very heart of golf, the very breath of its history on links that, for countless ages, have known so little change."

Pat Ward-Thomas, 1976

"At St. Andrews, you have a prideful shiver over first seeing the site of golf's genesis. It's to the golfer what The Vatican is to the Catholic, what Munich is to a beer drinker and what Mt. Everest is to the adventurer."

Hubert Mizell

"The visiting player must try to see the Old Course as it is . . . an area of links land where golf has been played endlessly for nigh on a thousand years."

James K. Robertson, 1967

"In my humble opinion, St. Andrews is the most fascinating golf course I have ever played."

Robert T. Jones, Jr.

"Nature was its only architect; its design owed little to the hand of man and has stood the test of centuries apart from occasional alterations as equipment became more powerful and sophisticated."

Pat Ward-Thomas

"I've never played well there. I have a difficult time picking out a target. I'd rather play a tight course with trees and very narrow fairways."

Hale Irwin, 1990

"If this isn't the grandest and greatest stage for any sporting event, I'll eat your gutta-percha."

Dick Taylor, 1990

"There are certain things you can't do here. You can't bang your clubs on the ground, or at least you feel like you can't."

Paul Azinger, 1990

"The Old Course is the finest in the world."

Seve Ballesteros

"St. Andrews never impressed me at all. I wondered how the devil it ever got the reputation. The only reason could be on account of its age."

"Wild Bill" Mehlhorn

"The more I studied the Old Course, the more I loved it and the more I loved it, the more I studied it."

Robert T. Jones, Jr.

"This is my favorite place in all the golfing world."

Jack Nicklaus

"If I had ever been set down in any one place and told I was to play there, and nowhere else for the rest of my life, I should have chosen the Old Course."

Robert T. Jones, Jr.

"The Old Course is so extraordinary—its subtleties beyond calculation, its mysteries unfathomable—that it defies conventional analysis."

Jim Finnegan, 1979

"You can play a damned good shot there and find the ball in a damned bad place."

George Duncan

"I have abiding respect for its strategic design, particularly the tight bunkering and variety in shape and slope of firm greens, and am intrigued by the uncluttered look and historic feel of the place."

William Campbell

"Never believe anybody who tells you he knows the Old Course inside-out. Only the dead really know St. Andrews."

Charles Price, 1980

"The fact that the Old Course is indisputably a 'classic'—and its bitterest enemies must at least concede it that—does not necessarily make it good, nor is it a reason why anyone should necessarily like it."

Henry Longhurst, 1955

"There is always a way at St. Andrews, although it is not always the obvious way, and in trying to find it, there is more to be learned on this British course than in playing a hundred ordinary American golf courses."

Robert T. Jones, Jr.

"How many courses start in the center of town and come back to the center? Not many. And it's the focal point of the whole town, really."

Jack Nicklaus, 1990

"I never thought I'd miss Pete Dye courses."

Scott Hoch, 1990

"If these pins were on these kinds of mounds and knobs at TPC courses, guys would be bellyaching, but here nothing bothers you."

Paul Azinger, 1990

"Every golf course in the world owes something to the Old Course for, either by accident or design, it embodies every feature and architectural trick."

Peter Dobereiner, 1982

"This is the great excellence of St. Andrews' links—the artful planting of the bunkers. Not, of course, that they were planted by any but Nature's hand—yet one would say with an obvious artistic eye for the golfer's edification."

Horace Hutchinson

"Nowhere in the world is golf so little cut and dried. It is a course of constant risks and constant opportunities of recovering, of infinitely varied and, to the stranger, unorthodox shots."

Bernard Darwin

"Say, that looks like an old abandoned golf course. What did they call it?"

Sam Snead, upon first seeing the Old Course from the train, 1946

"St. Andrews is the 'Mona Lisa' of golf courses."

Theodore Moone

"No course has commanded greater affection and respect from those who have learned to appreciate its subtleties and charms."

Pat Ward-Thomas

"There is only one Old Course and nature built it. It would be outright folly for any architect to attempt a duplication. The Old Course is only right at St. Andrews."

Robert Trent Jones

"When I first came to St. Andrews, I played one round and considered it the worst golf course I had ever seen. When I was here next, I played three days and I decided it was a good golf course. Next time I played all week and went away saying it was a great course. And now—I think it must be the most wonderful golf course in the world."

Ross Gardner, as captain of
the U.S. Walker Cup team,
1926

"You would be crucified if you built the Old Course at St. Andrews today, with all those hidden bunkers, enormous greens and fairways crossing each other."

Peter Alliss, 1981

"It's the worst golf hole in the world."

J. H. Taylor, referring to the
17th, or Road Hole

"St. Andrews has the most perfect golfing hazards which the mind can imagine, but even there these traps are not always successful in catching the bad shots; for the course contains too much good ground outside of the bunkers."

John L. Low, 1903

"After my third or fourth round I was an eloquent admirer of the Old Course."

Gene Sarazen

"St. Andrews is the ideal to aim at in all golf course construction. Fashions come and fashions go, but St. Andrews still remains a model of architecture at its best."

Peter Lawless

"I came here only last week and played over the course and I think it is the greatest course in the world."

Peter Thomson

"It is good in many respects, but the bunkers are badly placed. You get into them oftener with good shots than with bad ones. One or two need filling up and others making in different places. They punish the man who is driving well more than the man who is driving badly, for they are generally the length of a good drive."

Harry Vardon, 1905

"Frankly, I never liked St. Andrews and I never will. St. Andrews seems to get you that way, you either like it or hate it."

Norman von Nida, 1956

"I was impressed on my first visit to St. Andrews, the spiritual home of the game, by the scrupulous respect the ordinary players—the townspeople—had for the course."

Tony Lema, 1966

"The Old Course has probably had more effect on golf course architecture than any other single course."

Robert Trent Jones

"I could take out of my life everything except my experiences at St. Andrews and I would still have a rich full life."

Robert T. Jones, Jr.

SEMINOLE

"It affords everything I like best in golf."

Ben Hogan

"Here is one of the finest courses ever created. It meanders in places that are lower than the sea level and then are higher than a four-story building."

Roger Ganem, 1975

"When all is said and done, the course demands golf of the first order."

Herbert Warren Wind

"It is the only course I could be perfectly happy playing every single day."

Ben Hogan

"The intrinsic excellence of Seminole, with its premium on strategic thinking to avoid the gauntlet of bunkers and the large central lake which casts a powerful spell on the nervous, is matched by the immaculate condition of the course."

Peter Dobereiner, 1982

SHINNECOCK HILLS

"All in all I think it is one of the finest courses I have ever played."
Ben Hogan

"It has a link quality with tantalizing ocean breezes, natural rough and excellent par threes. It's a new course every day."
Jack Whitaker, 1979

SHOAL CREEK

"I think it's a very good layout, although I don't know if the rough has to be that tough."
Wayne Grady, 1990

"They ought to put red lines down either side of the fairway and call the rough lateral hazards."
Payne Stewart, 1990

"If they didn't have spotters out there, you'd never find your ball."
Tim Simpson, 1990

"Shoal Creek was an absolute joke. It was like playing on your local muni after a drought."
Curtis Strange, 1991

SOUTHERN HILLS

"It just doesn't look as tough as it is."

Byron Nelson

SPYGLASS HILL

"There is no doubt this is one of the prettiest pieces of land that has ever been butchered. It is a beautiful piece of land. Robert Trent Jones, Sr., has done some real nice courses, but this isn't one of them."

Lanny Wadkins, 1990

TPC AT SAWGRASS

"Too complicated."

Ben Crenshaw

"It'll be a fine course once you put in the greens."

Miller Barber

"All you can see is water."

Joe Inman

TURNBERRY

"Strangely enough, Turnberry is the only course on the rota of British Open venues—which consist only of links courses—where the ocean actually comes into play."

Greg Norman

Winged Foot

"Winged Foot has the toughest 18 finishing holes in golf."

Dave Marr, 1984

"The design of the course is superb. It has every conceivable type of hole."

Robert Sommers, 1974

"These greens are not small, but they play small because of the skill needed to hit to them in the right spots."

Jack Nicklaus, 1974

"The fellow who gets it up and down in two from those bunkers has to be playing with a prayer book in his pocket."

Fred Corcoran

6

Tournaments and Championships

Before the British Open was initiated in 1860, tournaments did not exist as we now know them. The early professionals played challenge matches with most of them being foursomes, or alternate shot formats, more popularly known in America as the Scotch foursome. Other tournaments followed in Great Britain, but not to the extent that a professional could make a living at it. The prize money was small. Professionals still caddied, made clubs or were keepers of the green if they, indeed, tried to make a living from golf.

The first open event in America was the 1895 U.S. Open and it really was a side show to the more important U.S. Amateur. It was a one-day affair with a field of 10 professionals and one amateur. Soon, other tournaments were established such as the Western, Metropolitan and North and South opens, but a regular tour didn't exist. The golf professional worked at a club. The tournaments were a chance to get together, play some golf and possibly win a little money. They were golf professionals first and players second. That is, until Walter Hagen.

The Haig was lured to Detroit and the big automobile dollars, becoming the professional at Oakland Hills. As the course was being built, there wasn't much to do except hit a few balls, take time off for a tournament or two, and have some fun talking with the members. That changed once the course was ready to play. Hagen wanted no part of repairing clubs or selling equipment, suggesting the club might want to hire Mike Brady, whom Hagen had defeated in a playoff for the 1919 U.S. Open. He virtually became the first professional golfer as opposed to a golf professional. The Haig was willing to take a chance on his ability as a player.

Winning titles was important, but only to help him book exhibitions and work out business deals with companies only too happy to have Hagen endorse their products. The important titles to Hagen were the British Open, U.S. Open and PGA Championship. If one eluded him, he would try for some other national championship like Canada, France or even Belgium. The first three were major championships, however, and were the goals of most professionals. With such outstanding amateur golfers as Jones, Evans, Ball, Hilton and Travers also winning national open championships, the British and U.S. amateurs were also thought of as major titles.

The golfing world now places a great deal of emphasis on the majors. They are, with one exception, championships, different than tournaments. The other major is the Masters, a championship of nothing and not even an open. It's really more of an invitational although certain standards have been set to determine who is eligible to compete. The Masters just sort of evolved as a major.

Perhaps the most important reason that it was set above other tournaments was the man behind it—Robert T. Jones, Jr. Rightfully, he was regarded by professionals, amateurs and golf fans everywhere as not only a great champion, but in every way, a gentleman. The person who ran the Masters was Clifford Roberts, seeing to every detail. Between Jones and Roberts, the tournament was run on a higher level than any other. The golf course was also outstanding. From the beginning, it was one of the finest layouts in the world, beautifully groomed and a pleasure to play. Remember in 1934, when the Masters started, most of the tour events were not played on the exclusive golf clubs in the country, but on public courses. In addition, Augusta National was not static. Improvements were made annually—a new tee here, a contour change on a green there and a mound added or leveled. Finally, the winners were mostly proven champions like Horton Smith, Gene Sarazen, Byron Nelson, Craig Wood, Sam Snead and Ben Hogan.

With the LPGA, it was easier. The powers that be in that organization simply declared that there would be four major events—the U.S. Women's Open and LPGA Championship, of which there was probably little argument, along with the Canadian Open and the Dinah Shore. No discussion, end of story.

The golfers who are best remembered are those who won the majors. There have been a number of good professionals who have won several tournaments during their careers, but are not placed in the same class as those who have major titles after their name. Harry Cooper is an example along with Ky Laffoon, Harold "Jug" McSpaden and Ed "Porky" Oliver.

Even when a golfer has won major titles, history may want more. The one which eluded Sam Snead, the U.S. Open, has been a blemish on his record even though he won every other major and is credited with 81 tour victories. Why, ask golfers, have Palmer and Watson been unable to win the PGA? Yet each has eight majors. Neither Byron Nelson nor Ray Floyd has won the British Open and both have said they would have dearly loved to have won that championship. The standard of winning each of the four majors will always be something to shoot at—only Gene Sarazen, Ben Hogan, Gary Player and Jack Nicklaus have accomplished that in modern times.

There is a huge difference in playing golf, tournament golf and championship golf. It is almost laughable to hear some amateur at a tournament try to make a comparison between his game and the professional he is watching. The same course is set up differently for a championship and some of the changes are very subtle. Let the rough grow, put the tees back and select certain pin positions and the three handicapper might be lucky to break 80.

In 1984, I presented the USGA with the two U.S. Open medals won by Walter Hagen. The head of the museum committee was Billy Joe Patton, the fine amateur who almost won the Masters. He invited me to play Oakland Hills with him on the Monday following the close of the championship and I quickly accepted. Nothing was changed from the final round as we used the same tees and pin positions from Sunday. Neither of us broke 90. In my case, that is no surprise, but Patton was still a fine player. The tournament player is so much better than the typical golfer, it's hard to make any comparison.

The LPGA Tour

"In the beginning a woman could get on the tour by just showing up. She would apply to join the LPGA and come out and play. She was either good enough to stay on tour or she wasn't."

Betsy Rawls, 1986

"We've been through a lot over the past few years and we've emerged as the best women's sports organization in the world."

Amy Alcott, 1991

"All the good players were losing their swings. All you had to do was bunt the ball."

JoAnne Carner, commenting on the short courses used for LPGA Tour in 1984

"I have a house to pay for."

Vicki Alvarez, on why she played in all but two 1985 LPGA events

"Sometimes when you're trying to make pars, that's the hardest score to make."

Betsy King, 1990

"The feminist movement never really touched the women's tour—we were all just totally unaware of it. I think that's because we were so involved in playing golf and winning tournaments."

Betsy Rawls, 1986

Collett-Vare

Carner

Didrikson

Lopez

Wright

L A D I E S

"My dad told me once that I'd lose a lot more tournaments than I'd win."

Nancy Lopez

"Sometimes the girls get angry because they don't get their pictures or their names in the papers. You can't put 100 women together without someone griping."

JoAnne Carner, talking
about the success of
Nancy Lopez on tour, 1979

THE PGA TOUR

"Take a thousand young boys and start them playing golf. Maybe one will emerge as a good enough player to think seriously about tournament golf as a career."

Peter Dobereiner, 1979

"It's the only sport in the world where the spectators can walk out to the pitcher's mound and talk to the pitcher."

Fred Corcoran

"Tournament golf can be heroic or tragic, a play of forces in which players and spectators alike may experience drama equal to that on any stage."

Robert T. Jones, Jr.

"They don't have any charisma and they do look alike. You say 'Hello' to them and they're stumped for an answer."

Miller Barber, on the crop of
young golfers on tour, 1985

"When I joined the tour in 1964, I told my wife I wanted to play five years. Instead, I've played five careers."

> **George Archer,** after 25 years on tour, 1989

"I thought about trying the tour, but I decided my long-hitting had more potential."

> **Evan "Big Cat" Williams,** twice National Long Drive champ

"If I'm going to play golf, I might as well play for money."

> **Arnold Palmer,** on turning pro, 1954

"Today, you have to prove yourself to get a PGA card. Back then, all you had to do was walk up, put up your dough and say, 'I'm a professional.'"

> **Johnny Revolta,** comparing the 1930's tour with today's, 1990

"Fellows, if I win tomorrow we will have champagne in here."

> **Tony Lema,** before final round of 1962 Orange County Open which he won and became known as "Champagne Tony"

"I'll see you down the road."

> Tony Lema, upon leaving the
> World Series of Golf in a
> private plane which crashed,
> killing him, 1966

"A player 45 to 50 can't realistically compete out here."

> David Graham, 1990

"Each time we play, we leave a little piece of ourselves on the course. You never know how much longer you'll be competitive."

> Dan Forsman, 1991

"Anybody who doesn't look at a scoreboard is crazy. I tell my caddie I want to know where I stand and what the guys near me are doing."

> Hale Irwin

"In every tournament there is a key shot."

> Ben Hogan

"I just hope the guys on tour don't rib him too much. You know, losing to a woman. The ones who do will be those who were too wimpy to play."

> Julie Inkster, after winning the
> Spalding Invitational Pro-Am
> by a stroke over Mark Brooks,
> becoming the first woman to win
> in a field of men and women pros,
> 1991

"The only stats I care about are paychecks and victories."
                                                    Greg Norman, 1988

"There's no use going out there when you have to try to try."
                                                    Byron Nelson

"By almost every yardstick, the American PGA Tour is the finest golf circuit in the world, and by a long way."
                                                    Peter Dobereiner, 1981

"If Hogan brought dignity and new gate appeal to the professional game, it remained for Arnie Palmer to carry it into the living rooms and lay it in the laps of the ladies of the house."
                                                    Will Grimsley, 1976

"Patience was the main thing I had to learn when I went out on the Tour."
                                                    Arnold Palmer, 1980

"You don't really make your money playing on the golf Tour. I've just been fortunate in that I've received opportunities as a result of how well I've played through the years. It's the outside interests where I make my living."
                                                    Jack Nicklaus, 1979

"In 20 years of tournament golf involving amateurs, I've never been hit by a ball."

> Hale Irwin, at Pebble Beach
> one week before being hit in
> the forehead at the
> Los Angeles Open, 1989

"My guess is that golf gained its rightful place in the sports world when Sam Snead beat Ben Hogan in a playoff at the 1954 Masters championship. The two greatest players in head-to-head competition gained the fancy of the public."

> **Bob Drum**

"Every time you miss a four-footer out there it puts a bullet hole in you. After 14 years, I felt like I'd been machine-gunned."

> **Joe Inman**

"This is a job for me. We could go out right now with a six-pack and a cart and play 18 holes and we'd have a pretty good time. But once you start playing in front of 30,000 people, under all that pressure, it's not fun."

> **Dave Hill**

"To win golf tournaments, you have to be right both physically and mentally. And then confidence gives you the extra boost that's required to win."

> **Tom Watson**

"We have the best officials in all sport. You don't see them until you need them."

> **Jerry Pate**

"Even under the grubbiest conditions, it is impossible to play the Tour without spending $20,000 a year."

Mark Mulvoy, 1980

"I never did make money playing the tour. It cost me more, total, than my purse winnings. I had to do other things."

Ben Hogan

"It's nice to know I'm going to have a job 10 years from now."

Roger Maltbie, following
victory in the 1985
World Series of Golf, giving
him a 10-year tour exemption

"Of the 10 leading money winners in 1953 only one, Cary Middlecoff, went to college, while in 1963 eight of the 10 leaders had."

Tony Lema

"Great. I opened my locker and there were a dozen new shirts, boxes of balls and two pair of golf shoes. Now that I can afford them, they give them to me."

Paul Azinger

"I keep hearing that golf's top money men and stars are biting the hand that feeds them by not showing up in tournaments. How many tournaments do they expect a guy to play in, anyway? You just can't go on from week to week and give a top performance."

Arnold Palmer

"The golf course is the greatest office in the world—six miles of fresh air."

Chi Chi Rodriguez

"A good teaching professional can teach a young man to hit a golf ball with a stick pretty near perfectly every time, but how do you teach that man to hit that tiny ball with a whippy stick when 15,000 people are jammed around him like a crowd at a six-alarm fire, when several million eyes are peering at him on television and when $250,000 is riding directly or indirectly, on the next shot he hits?"

Tony Lema

"I don't care how they know me—ability, jumping in the lake or orange golf balls, just as long as they know me."

Jerry Pate

"I lost more tournaments than I won."

Ben Hogan

"It's so satisfying to win over here, because it's so hard to do. It puts you on a different level to win on the American Tour."

Ken Brown, British golf
professional, following victory
in the Southern Open, 1987

"My only fear is that I may have to go out and get a real job."

Fuzzy Zoeller

Nelson

Sarazen

Watson

Trevino

GREATS

"I enjoy the last two days of a tournament a lot more than the first two. There's more riding on it."

Greg Norman

"Tournaments are won on Sunday and on the back nine."

Jack Nicklaus

"Probably only those who have experienced it can ever really realize the strain involved in tournament golf."

Bobby Locke, 1953

SENIOR TOUR

"I've been out here 33 years, but this is like starting over again with a new career."

Gary Player, 1985

"Our tour is based on nostalgia, on bringing back the heroes of 25 years ago."

Frank Beard, 1991

"If I retired, all I'd do is play golf and go fishing. That's what I'm doing now."

Julius Boros, 1985

"No, I always considered myself a junior."

Ben Hogan, replying to a
question as to whether he ever
considered playing the
Senior Tour

"I'm going to play as many tournaments as I can. If you don't see my name on the entry list you'll know I'm sick."

Gibby Gilbert, 1991

"We're the round-bellies and we don't hit it as far as the flat-bellies, but we get it around pretty well, and, my God, do we laugh."

Lee Trevino

"I want to break every record on the Senior Tour."

Chi Chi Rodriguez

"What I need is a tour for guys over 70."

Sam Snead, 1981

"They'd have to carry me out of here before they would get me in a golf cart."

Arnold Palmer, when carts were permitted on the Senior Tour for the first time, 1985

"I've set a goal for myself to win on both the regular and senior tours this year. When I can no longer play the regular tour, then I'll enjoy playing senior golf."

Jack Nicklaus, 1990

"Nicklaus faces a big challenge when he comes out here. Never mind his job of winning on the regular tour. He's going to have a big enough job winning out here."

Gary Player, 1990

"Not again. We've already done that for 21 years."

Jimmye Aaron, wife of
Tommy, when informed he
would join the Senior Tour

"The one thing I see on this tour is that we don't have a beer stand every other hole. About 5 p.m., they're getting a little rowdy on the other tour."

Lee Trevino, 1990

"When you stand on the practice tee everybody else has gray hair, too."

Larry Mowry

"It's golf's greatest mulligan."

Lee Trevino

THE MAJORS

"We all say majors are just another 72-hole tournament. In a way, they are, but we're really just saying that to keep ourselves from getting too fired up."

Curtis Strange, 1990

"I don't think people fully appreciate how hard we work, and mentally how hard it is to win a major."

Nick Faldo, 1989

"The time is long overdue for official golfdom to clean up its 'act'—the act of pretending that the national amateur championships of the United States and Great Britain are 'major' tournaments worthy of a place alongside the U.S. Open, British Open, The Masters and PGA Championship."

Richard V. Levin, 1978

"It's a great feeling winning a major. I can't imagine what Jack Nicklaus feels like winning 20."

Jeff Sluman, winning the
PGA Championship, 1988

"Someone will break my record someday, but I want that number to be higher than it is now."

Jack Nicklaus, 1979, with 17
majors. He increased the
record to 20.

"Majors are for the younger guys."

Miller Barber, commenting
on which senior events might
be considered majors

"I'm 24 and I think I'll get a lot more opportunities."

Jerry Pate, after losing the
1978 PGA in a playoff. He
never won another major after
the 1976 U.S. Open.

"I would like to see a major championship played someday with no fairways. I would have a very good chance to win."

Seve Ballesteros

"I once asked Jack Nicklaus which of his 18 majors was the best and he said they were all the best. I didn't believe him at the time, but I do now."

> **Nick Faldo**, after winning the
> the 1990 British Open, his
> fourth major

U.S. OPEN

"Whoever wins the Open next Sunday, whether it is an unknown or an established player, whoever wins it, treat it well, because the U.S. Open Championship is the greatest championship in golf."

> **Ken Venturi**, 1969

"The U.S. Open is the toughest tournament to win."

> **Tom Watson**, 1990

"I am as much surprised and as pleased as anyone here. Naturally it was always my hope to win out. I simply tried my best to keep this cup from going to our friends across the water. I am very glad to have been the agency for keeping the cup in America."

> **Francis Ouimet**, upon
> accepting the U.S. Open
> trophy after defeating
> Harry Vardon and Ted Ray in
> the playoff, 1913

"It's not so much that Hogan did it, but that others haven't done it, the great Arnold Palmer, Jack Nicklaus, Tom Watson."

> **Curtis Strange**, after winning
> his second consecutive
> U.S. Open, 1989

"There's no hiding the fact that we all know what is at stake. Since the Masters, it pretty much has consumed me, thinking about it."

> **Curtis Strange,** 1990, on trying to become only the second in history to win three consecutive U.S. Opens

"When I won at Medinah, I didn't have any idea what winning the Open would mean to my career."

> **Cary Middlecoff,** 1990

"Gary Player has as much a chance of winning the U.S. Open as I have of beating Mike Tyson in a heavyweight fight."

> **Dave Hill,** discussing Player's exemption in the 1990 championship

"Honoring the old champions by letting them play is a trip down nostalgia lane. If in 1999 I were given a special exemption, I would respectfully decline."

> **Hale Irwin,** 1985. He won in 1990, giving him a 10-year exemption through 2000.

"Each time Ainsley missed the ball, the current would sweep it farther downstream and he would have to run along behind it, trying to get in a decisive blow. No man ever showed more gameness."

> **Henry McLemore,** on Ray Ainsley's record 19 strokes on one hole at Cherry Hills, 1938

"I thought I had to play the ball as it lay at all times."

> **Ray Ainsley,** explaining why
> he didn't take a drop and a
> penalty stroke, 1938

"Do they dig chuck holes at the Indianapolis 500?"

> **Dave Hill,** referring to course
> preparation at the Open

"There goes the Grand Slam for another year."

> **Arnold Palmer,** after losing
> to Nicklaus in 1962

"To be considered a truly great player, you must win the Open."

> **Tom Watson,** prior to his
> victory, 1980

"I'd like to be out there in the rain at Oakland Hills. I still have trouble believing they are playing without me."

> **Arnold Palmer,** 1985, after
> failing to qualify for the Open
> and not being given an
> exemption which would have
> tied Sarazen's record for
> consecutive appearances

"No, sir, it's the first time."

> **Orville Moody,** responding to
> President Nixon's remark that
> it wasn't very often a man
> spends 14 years in the Army
> and then comes out to win the
> U.S. Open

"Every time you make a par in the U.S. Open, you're passing a lot more guys than are passing you."

Lou Graham, 1980

"Snead must win the big one early or he'll never win it at all. This was his great chance. From now on, each Open will become progressively harder for Sam."

Gene Sarazen, after Snead
finished second to
Ralph Guldahl, 1937

"If I'd won that first Open, I'd have probably won it eight times."

Sam Snead, who never won
the U.S. Open

"I think they put too much emphasis on it, too much prestige."

Sam Snead

"I won this tournament once when I really wasn't supposed to and four other times I lost when I should have won. I guess things balance out."

Arnold Palmer

"Victory is everything. You can spend the money, but you can never spend the memories."

Ken Venturi

"I could not win this tournament. This course is too big for me. Twenty-eight thousand yards of slugging would be too much for me. I haven't the physical endurance and I only hope to play well."

> **Cyril Walker,** prior to the
> championship held at
> Oakland Hills which he won by
> three strokes over Jones, 1924

"The difference between the Masters and the U.S. Open is the difference between fun and fear."

> **Tony Lema**

"A man must be lucky to win the U.S. Open."

> **Willie Macfarlane,** the 1925
> champion

"That's right, Willie, if you win it only once."

> **Walter Hagen,** two-time
> champion

"I thought I had won at Pebble Beach. And I think my season more or less ended there. I got myself up and did what I thought I needed to do. Obviously the shot Tom (Watson) made knocked me down. I haven't played well since."

> **Jack Nicklaus,** 1982

"I'm not going to get the ball close, I'm going to sink it."

> **Tom Watson,** to caddie
> Bruce Edwards before holing
> his chip on the 71st hole,
> virtually locking up the 1982
> title

"You little S.O.B., I am really proud of you."

> **Jack Nicklaus,** to Watson
> after Tom's 1982 victory

"The name is Hagen. I've come down from Rochester to help you fellows stop Vardon and Ray."

> **Walter Hagen,** to other
> Americans in the locker room
> at The Country Club, 1913

"Don't worry about me. When I come up the 18th fairway for the second time tomorrow you'll think you're seeing another Jesse Owens."

> **Ben Hogan,** before the final
> two rounds at Merion, 1950

"I still know every shot I hit, and how I got around."

> **Jack Fleck,** 1980, recalling
> his 1955 victory

"I'm just trying to build up as big a lead as I can so I won't choke."

> **Lee Trevino,** at the 71st hole
> in the championship at
> Oak Hill, 1968

"I may buy the Alamo and give it back to the Mexicans."

> **Lee Trevino,** when asked how
> he was going to spend the
> $30,000 winner's check, 1968

"I made a promise to myself after the 1962 Open that if God ever gave me the privilege of winning this title, I would donate the purse to a good cause."

> **Gary Player,** who donated the $25,000 he won to junior golf and cancer research, 1965

"If I'd missed that putt and lost a tournament already won, I hate to think of what might have happened to my confidence.

> **Robert T. Jones, Jr.,** regarding his final putt to tie Al Espinosa, 1929 (Jones went on to win the playoff by 23 strokes.)

BRITISH OPEN

"My first regret is that I didn't make more of an effort to win the British Open."

> **Byron Nelson**

"Right now, I'd trade 'em all, all my regular tour wins, for the British Open."

> **Ray Floyd,** needing only the British Open to win all four majors

"I enjoy just being at the British Open, because of the unique atmosphere. It's stodgy, as only Britain can be, and yet there is a casual and almost festive feeling about the tournament."

> **Hubert Green,** 1980

HOGAN

"From 1924 to 1930, except in one single year, the Open Championship was won by Walter Hagen or Bobby Jones."

Bernard Darwin, 1944

"I wasn't going to lose this one by doing something stupid."

Nick Faldo, after shooting 18 consecutive pars in the final round at Muirfield, 1987

"It's too much to comprehend. I'm the British Open champion. It's something that will stay with you. Think of all the great people who have won. All the tradition."

Bill Rogers

"I be very happy to have this cup today. I work so hard for it, so many years."

Roberto de Vicenzo, at the presentation ceremonies, 1967

"I won the other tournament."

Hubert Green, after finishing eight behind winner Watson and seven behind Nicklaus, both of whom broke the Open scoring record, 1977

"In a way I don't feel great about it. But I hope Nicklaus wins the PGA Championship. Then I'll be known not just as the British Open champion, but as the man who stopped the Grand Slam."

> **Lee Trevino,** after Nicklaus won the Masters and U.S. Open, but was second in the British Open, 1972 (Nicklaus was never a factor in the 1972 PGA.)

"I don't want a second. If I can't win I don't care where I finish."

> **Walter Hagen,** to H. B. Martin after an opening 85, 1920 (Martin suggested Hagen try to play for second place.)

"I'll be back."

> **Walter Hagen,** after finishing 53rd in his first start, 1920

"I have never—I mean never—played better golf."

> **Arnold Palmer,** finishing 67–69 to win at Troon in horrible weather, 1961

"I was called by Walter Hagen, Tommy Armour and Bobby Cruickshank. They told me I had to go over there and play, even though I might not win, to complete my career."

> **Ben Hogan,** 1976

"Are you sure you played all the holes, Christy?"

> **Henry Cotton,** when
> Christy O'Connor shot 64 in
> 1985 to break Cotton's course
> record set 51 years earlier

"I've always said I would play as long as I felt I was competitive and enjoyed it. This week I wasn't competitive and didn't enjoy it."

> **Jack Nicklaus,** 1987

"Well, it's a step in the right direction."

> **Sandy Lyle,** responding to a
> newsman after winning when
> asked, "You've been criticized
> in the past for not playing up
> to your potential. Do you
> think this will stop all that?",
> 1985

PGA CHAMPIONSHIP

"No matter how hard you scratch it, you're not going to get my name off that trophy and I'm just happy to have it there."

> **Wayne Grady,** 1990

"You can take the titles to the grave, but you can't take the money."

> **Gene Sarazen,** 1991

"Can I become a semi-known, now?"

> **Dave Stockton,** referring to
> newspaper articles calling him
> an unknown when he was
> leading the PGA after three
> rounds, 1970

"The PGA is hardly to be considered in ranking to the other three."

> **Peter Dobereiner,** 1970

"Which one of you is going to be the runner-up?"

> **Walter Hagen** to Al Watrous,
> Bill Mehlhorn and Leo Diegel
> in locker room prior to the
> championship, 1925 (He beat
> all three en route to the title.)

"You know he's going to beat me. I don't know how he can do it, but he's going to do it."

> **Leo Diegel** to Frank Walsh
> when Diegel was two up with
> two holes to play, 1925
> (Hagen won on the 39th hole.)

British Amateur

"Never since the days of Caesar has the British nation been subjected to such humiliation."

> **Lord Northbourne,** at the
> presentation ceremonies after
> Walter Travis became the first
> American to win, 1904

THE MASTERS

"Masters Sunday, there is no other day in golf like it."

Dick Taylor, 1990

"I feel as though I'm a part of this place. As long as I'm alive, I'll come up here."

Gene Sarazen, at the age of 88, in 1990

"This is an invitational tournament, and the field, generally in the neighborhood of 80-odd players, has no more than 20 competitors with a real chance of winning."

Oscar Fraley, 1978

"At Augusta, history is the biggest thing. There are so many people who grew up dreaming about winning the Masters. You know you are going to be immortalized if you win it. It's got more to do with history and green jackets and azaleas than playing the course."

Dr. Bob Rotells, sports psychologist, on the pressure of winning, 1990

"I can't tell you what this means to me. It is so sweet. The sweetest moment of my life. Thank God my dad was here to see it."

Ben Crenshaw, 1984

"I hope to God they don't send me another invitation. I don't want to be here."

Lee Trevino, 1986

"They're making the greens as hard as marble and whoever gets the lucky bounces wins this week."

Fuzzy Zoeller, 1988

"I have never felt so tiny, so insignificant, so alone. The way people cheered, the stands, the noise, the bustle, the colours, the blinding sunshine, the sheer Americaness of the whole thing—I just felt completely out of it, a very small fish in an enormous ocean."

Peter Alliss, 1988, about his Masters appearance in 1966

"The best golf I've ever seen for a single stretch was the playoff at the 1979 Masters between Eddie Sneed, Tom Watson and Fuzzy Zoeller."

Ken Venturi, 1980

"It's the easiest cut to make of the year; you've got 80-some players and a lot of them don't even belong there."

Lee Trevino

"There is not one golfer in the world who can honestly say that the Masters is a major championship."

Tommy Bolt, 1971

"They started something at the Masters in 1935 that is very common today, but back then it was kind of a novelty. On the first tee each player was given a chart showing the pin placements on each green, so that on blind second shots the player didn't have to walk up ahead to see the green."

Gene Sarazen

"I don't want to take anything away from Larry Mize, but I think it is more likely that the real champion will win in an 18-hole playoff."

> **Seve Ballesteros,** after his
> sudden-death playoff loss to
> Larry Mize in 1987

"The field here, frankly, is one of the weakest we play in all year."

> **Frank Beard,** 1974

"Odds are about 100 to 1 against it, because so few are in the field. Eventually a foreigner will win it."

> **Gene Sarazen,** 1960 (It did
> happen the very next year
> when Player won and has
> become a regular occurrence.)

"We are a little surprised as well as being flattered that 18 Congressmen would be able to take time out to help us operate a golf tournament."

> **Clifford Roberts,** in response
> to a telegram suggesting
> Lee Elder should be invited to
> play, 1973

"As soon as a black golfer becomes eligible for an invitation under the qualifying system he will be welcome at Augusta just like anyone else."

> **Clifford Roberts,** 1973

"I will definitely accept an invitation to the Masters and I will definitely play in the Masters. I didn't have to weigh it very heavily. It is something I have always wanted."

> **Lee Elder,** following a victory
> in the Monsanto Open, 1974

"Cliff and I have decided you will have to put the coat on yourself."

> **Robert T. Jones, Jr.,** to Nicklaus when he became the first to repeat as champion. The tradition is for the defending champion to help the winner on with his jacket.

"I'd dream of winning the Masters, but I'd never dreamed of winning it like this."

> **Larry Mize,** who made a 30-yard chip on the second playoff hole against Greg Norman in 1987

"My hands were shaking so badly on the first tee, I was just hoping I would be able to tee my ball up."

> **Ray Floyd,** about his first appearance

"From the first time I played there, I felt it was a tournament I could win."

> **Arnold Palmer**

"They have little regard for the feelings of anybody, save a few special players who write them nice letters after the tournament is over telling them what a delightful show they put on."

> **Tommy Bolt**

"Billy Joe Patton almost certainly would have won if he had managed to restrain his enthusiasm on those two par-five holes."

> Robert T. Jones, Jr., discussing Patton's double-bogey on 13 and bogey on 15, leaving him one stroke behind Snead and Hogan, 1954

"I am a stupid."

> Roberto de Vicenzo, after signing for an incorrect score, costing him a chance to be in a playoff with Bob Goalby, 1968

"I'll be back every year if I have to walk fifteen hundred miles to do it."

> Herman Keiser, following his victory, 1946

"This is the only course I know where you choke when you come in the gate."

> Lionel Hebert

THE DOUBLE EAGLE

"So there was the great tournament, all tied up, with a playoff at 36 holes the next day, by one of the greatest shots of history—the greatest, I assume, that anyone in that huge gallery had ever seen in the pinch of real competition; perhaps the greatest shot ever played."

> O. B. Keeler

"You need four 3s, Mister Gene, 3–3–3–3."

> Stovepipe, Sarazen's caddie,
> when asked what he needed to
> catch Craig Wood at the 15th
> hole

"We were followed by a sparse gallery."

> Gene Sarazen, although
> thousands have claimed to
> have witnessed the shot

"Hurry up, will ya, I've got a date tonight."

> Walter Hagen, who was
> paired with Sarazen, just
> before the famous shot

"I took my stance with my four-wood and rode into the shot with every ounce of strength and timing I could muster. The split second I hit the ball I knew it would carry the pond. It tore for the flag on a very low trajectory, no more than 30 feet in the air."

> Gene Sarazen

"Sarazen just put his right foot back and hit a low hooking shot. Just the wrong kind of shot for the circumstance."

> Frank Walsh, 1986

"When Gene hit his second shot with a spoon I was standing on a mound about 50 yards away. His swing into the ball was so perfect and free, one knew immediately that it was a gorgeous shot."

> Robert T. Jones, Jr.

"That double-eagle wouldn't have meant a thing if I hadn't won the playoff the next day."

                                                            Gene Sarazen

"The aspect of the double-eagle that I cherish most is that both Walter Hagen and Bobby Jones witnessed the shot."

                                                            Gene Sarazen

THE GRAND SLAM

"He's simply too good. He'll go to Britain and win the Amateur and the Open, and then he'll come back over here and win the Open and the Amateur. He is playing too well to be stopped this year."

                              Bobby Cruickshank, early in
                              1930 (He backed up his
                              prediction by betting on Jones
                              with a British bookie and won
                              a great deal of money.)

"The Grand Slam has been called the greatest single record in golf, and it would be foolish to even try to think of a greater one."

                                                            Charles Price, 1980

"The Grand Slam cannot be broken and it will be tied long about the time women are running the four-minute mile."

                                                            Herbert Warren Wind

"The public could not immediately grasp what Jones had done because the Grand Slam was ethereal."

                                                            Charles Price, 1986

"If ever a man looked done it was Bobby in the last round when he took seven to the eighth hole and an old lady with a broom stick could have got a five from the spot where Bobby had reached in two. But he pulled himself together and finished like a lion and the others fell down."

Bernard Darwin, describing
Jones's victory in the Open

"The record is safely entrenched—I make bold to say this—for all time, in the Impregnable Quadrilateral of Golf."

O. B. Keeler, 1931

THE MODERN GRAND SLAM

"What if a guy were to win the Masters, the U.S. and British Opens and the PGA. That would be a Grand Slam."

Arnold Palmer, in what was
the first reference to the
Modern Grand Slam, 1960

7

Caddies

I fondly remember my early caddie days. Being a caddie not only introduced me to the wonderful game and afforded me the opportunity to play, but it also shaped my life. I was like that kid in the television commercial that I have only seen run during the Masters, standing with a bag on his shoulder and watching a member drive into the club in a shiny Cadillac. The commercial had only one word and it came from the young boy. Watching that car, he said, "Someday." That's how I felt. I wanted to be like some of the members, dress nicely and have good equipment. And when I played at my club, my caddie would be treated like a partner.

Unfortunately, there are fewer and fewer caddies, at least in the United States. There are still some organizations, most notably the Western Golf Association, trying to keep the role of the caddie an important part of golf. Scholarships like the Evans Scholars program, started by the great amateur Chick Evans, are offered to those who qualify with contributions coming from member clubs and other programs. I have had the pleasure of being a part of the scholarship selection process. It's a wonderful experience to be briefed on the candidates' high school records and then have a chance to talk with them and hear their hopes for the future.

American caddies are generally young. They leave the ranks for better-paying jobs or to further their education, and that's the way it should be. The situation is different in other countries. During a tournament at Chantilly, outside Paris, my caddie was a delightful grandmother. I was concerned about the weight of my golf bag and I arranged to borrow a lighter one after the first practice round. My caddie would have no part of it, returning to the storage area and putting all of my clubs back in my bag. She played every shot with me and when I was lucky enough to win, she walked off the 72nd hole beaming and gave me a big hug.

The lady who was my caddie in Japan had a motorized cart which moved with the touch of a button. When I took a divot, she had a bucket filled with soil and grass seed that was immediately applied to the scar in the ground. The only English she knew was, "Nice par," which I heard all too infrequently. Still, we had no problem communicating, mostly by hand signals.

In Scotland, my favorite caddie was Jock, a youngster of 72. The other caddies told me he was the caddie champion of all those who worked at Muirfield. He took great pleasure in my shots that day and I performed to his satisfaction. Later, while we were at a pub with the caddies, we discovered they had bet among themselves and Jock made out pretty well. The result was that we not only picked up the tab for drinks and lunch, but each golfer made sure his caddie received his fees all over again so they wouldn't go home emptyhanded. I got the impression they may have gone home with nothing in their pockets anyway, because they were still at the pub when we departed.

On a trip to Bermuda, I had a caddie named Ralph when playing Riddle's Bay. After the round he asked if I would be playing the next day and I told him I had a starting time at Mid-Ocean at 10 in the morning. When I arrived, there was Ralph. I have no idea what kind of arrangement he made with the caddiemaster, but I was pleased he was there. As we started, I took off my watch, asking if he would keep it for me until the end of the round. When we were finished, our group sat at the clubhouse enjoying a drink when someone asked about the time. It was then I realized my watch had not been returned and we had been sitting there for at least an hour. I was reasonably sure my watch was gone, but I went down to the caddie area where I was met by the caddiemaster, asking if he could be of service. Hardly two words were out of my mouth when he produced an envelope. On it was my name and the hotel where I was staying along with a note from Ralph.

There is a partnership between caddie and golfer—hard to explain, but easy to feel—the golfer knows immediately if he has a good caddie or just a club-carrier. I know that I felt part of every win "my man" had more than 40 years ago and I hope my caddies feel the same.

———

"If ever a man can be a guide, philosopher, and friend to his master, that man is the golf caddie."

Henry Longhurst, 1937

"A caddie, as a rule, is about as good a caddie as the disposition of his employer."

Grantland Rice, 1926

"Don't forget the caddies, gentlemen. The players get the glory or the sting of defeat. But they don't do all the fighting."

O. B. Keeler

"The traditional St. Andrews caddie, from whom sprang the original professionals of the game, has always taken his duties with the seriousness due to gowff."

James K. Robertson, 1967

"So well versed were the caddies in the game and so acquainted with your own weaknesses, that they would hand you the club you ought to play with, and should you refuse it and take one of your own choice, you would usually make a bad shot. The refusal to take the club your caddy chose seemed to have a psychological influence over you."

Charles Blair Macdonald,
commenting on the caddies of
St. Andrews, 1928

"Make friends with your caddie and the game will make friends with you."

Stephen Potter, 1948

"The way most golfers tell it, St. Andrews' caddies are the world's best and can read the grass right down to the roots from Burn Hole, which is No. 1 on the Old Course, to Home Hole. Mine were a bunch of bums."

Sam Snead

"He was far more useful to me than a club. Without his help I doubt if I could have won it. It amazed me the way he just put the club in my hand."

Tony Lema, about
Tip Anderson, Jr., his caddie
in the British Open, 1964

"When I won the Masters, the caddie I had that week told me, 'If you want to win the Masters, you listen to me.' I told him, 'If you want to keep carrying a bag, shut up.' He said, 'Yes, boss.'"

George Archer

"The first-class player, it may broadly be said, always has a caddie—and has done so since the game began."

Henry Longhurst, 1937

"The caddie in golf occupies a position accorded to the attendants in no other game and paralleled only by the relationship of squire to knight in the lists."

Robert Browning

CADDIES

"Some caddies are teetotalers, but not many."

Andra Kirkaldy

"With Carl, it's almost like he's playing the round with you."

Ben Crenshaw, referring to
Carl Jackson who first caddied
for him in the 1976 Masters

"When you see a player miss a shot, one of the first things they do is get mad at their caddie."

Deborah McHaffie

"If you want to see the girl caddie at her finest, you must go to Japan."

Henry Longhurst

"D'ye see yon man? D'ye ken the best club in his set—it's his pencil."

"Old" Crawford, caddie at
North Berwick

"I started at a dime for fore-caddie work, then a quarter as a caddie. But I got big tips because I had clever toes and my man never had a bad lie."

Chi Chi Rodriguez, 1990

"I don't know why someone would want to give up a $75,000-a-year job to go to school for four years to get a job making $20,000."

Orville Moody, talking about
his daughter, Michelle, who
caddied for him on the
Senior Tour instead of going
to college

"My, but you're a wonder, sir."

> The caddie for R. T. Jones, Jr.,
> when he played a round at the
> Old Course, 1936

"The golfer who does not take a caddie at St. Andrews denies himself the wine of the country."

> Herbert Warren Wind

"Though the henchman who carries your clubs may be a most able adviser, you will seldom, as a beginner, derive much encouragement from his criticism."

> Horace Hutchinson, 1886

"If I could have caddied for Sam Snead nobody else would have ever won a tournament."

> Ben Hogan

"What's the matter, boss, you getting a little tight?"

> Nathaniel "Ironman" Avery,
> to Arnold Palmer in 1964 Masters

"You can get fined for throwing a golf club. I don't think there's a fine for throwing a caddie."

> Tommy Bolt

"She is the only caddie I know who gets 100 percent of the purse."

> **Mark Calcavecchia,** on what
> it's like having his wife caddie
> for him on tour, 1991

"The golfer as a rule gets as good a caddie as he deserves to get. Most of the time even better."

> **Grantland Rice,** 1926

"The bond between a golfer and caddie, to me, is one of the most enjoyable relationships that can exist between employer and employee."

> **Henry Longhurst**

"Some clubs have 'A' caddies and 'B' caddies. The only way you can tell them apart is that the 'A's cost more than the 'B's."

> **Robinson Murray,** 1951

"You must always remember that the average caddie is a far better golfer than you; and, therefore, by simple logic he feels he should be the one playing golf and you should be carrying the bag."

> **Stephen Baker,** 1962

"There are perhaps a million boys caddying: you as an adult can set them a good or bad example in life by your etiquette and observance of the rules of the game."

> **Gene Sarazen**

"Caddying can be pleasant work for a boy, and you can help yourself a great deal by treating him as a fellow man who also enjoys the game."

> **Lealand Gustavson,** 1954

"To break clubs over one's knees is a sign of weakness. The really strong-minded golfer breaks them over his caddie's back."

Ralph Moore, in the
Denver Post, 1971

"The player may experiment about his swing, his grip, his stance. It is only when he begins asking his caddie's advice that he is getting on dangerous ground."

Sir W. G. Simpson

8

Playing By the Rules

The world of golf operated under one set of rules for a great many years until the formation of the United States Golf Association in 1894. The rules came from the Royal and Ancient Golf Club of St. Andrews, although that was not always so and that august group was not the first to set guidelines for golfers. That distinction belongs to the Honourable Company of Edinburgh Golfers.

Originally there were 13 rules, brief and easy to understand, that is if you were playing golf in 1744. They were signed by John Rattray, captain of the Gentlemen Golfers. No mention was made of penalties if the rules were broken. Apparently gentlemen golfers didn't break the rules.

I You must tee your ball within one club's length of the hole.

II Your tee must be upon the ground.

III You are not to change the ball you strike off the tee.

IV You are not to remove Stones, Bones or any Break Club, for the sake of playing your Ball, except upon the Fair Green and that only within a Club's length of your Ball.

V If your Ball come among watter or any wattery filth, you are at liberty to take out your Ball and bringing it behind the hazard and teeing it, you may play it with any club and allow your Adversary a Stroke, for so getting out your ball.

VI If your balls be found anywhere touching one another you are to lift the first ball, till you play the last.

VII At Holing, you are to play your Ball honestly for the Hole, and not play upon your Adversary's Ball, not lying in your way to the Hole.

VIII If you should lose your Ball, by its being taken up, or any other way you are to go back to the Spot, where you struck last, and drop another Ball, and allow your Adversary a Stroke for the misfortune.

IX No man at Holing his Ball is to be allowed, to mark his way to the Hole with his Club or anything else.

X If a Ball be stopp'd by any person, Horse, Dog or anything else, the Ball so stopp'd must be play'd where it lyes.

XI If you draw your Club, in order to Strike and proceed to far in the Stroke, as to be bringing down your Club: if then your Club shall break, in any way, it is to be Accounted a Stroke.

XII He whose Ball lyes farthest from the Hole is obliged to play first.

XIII Neither Trench, Ditch or Dyke, made for the presentation of the Links, nor the Scholar's Holes or the Soldier's Lines, Shall be accounted a Hazard. But the Ball is to be taken out and Tee'd and play'd with any Iron Club.

The last rule was a local one to take into account the conditions at the links during that time. The other 12, however, were the basis for rules adopted by other clubs.

Because of the complexity of the game and the different fields of play, more were added and interpretations of existing rules were necessary. Initially, the rules set forth by the USGA followed those of the R & A, but circumstances dictated some differences as the years passed. One occurred following the stunning victory by Walter Travis in the 1904 British Amateur.

Travis was born in Australia but in reality was an American and it was in that capacity that he entered the championship. Not a long hitter, Travis won match after match with deft approaching and putting. He was not very popular with the British, which was probably caused by incidents on both sides. Travis was a grim, no-nonsense type of man who felt he was not being treated fairly by the British and let them know his feelings. The British, on the other hand, were not very pleased that an American invader was beating their best amateur golfers. They blamed the putter being used by Travis, not wishing to give any credit for his skills on the greens. It was a Schenectady model with a center shaft and a mallet head.

Following Travis' victory, the R & A passed a rule banning center shaft putters. Ironically, shortly after the championship, he abandoned using it since it seemed to have lost its magic. The ban stayed in the rules for nearly 50 years, until lifted prior to the 1953 season. That was the year Ben Hogan entered the British Open for the first time and won—using a center shaft putter.

Eventually the R & A and the USGA got together to agree on one set of rules for golfers all over the world. Each has a committee and they meet biennially to discuss changes and additions. Unlike other sports, golf has no referees or umpires. Golfers police their own actions on the course. It is truly a gentleman's game.

———

"The game is not worth playing unless the rules are strictly followed."
James Braid

"Running through the Rules are underlying principles, that, like the steel rods which lie below the surface of reinforced concrete, serve to bind together the brittle material and to give it strength."
Richard S. Tufts, 1960

"The rules are based on three fundamental principles: That the golfer must play the ball as it lies, play the course as he finds it, and finally, where neither of the first two principles can apply, settle all questions by fair play."

Joseph C. Dey, Jr., 1956

"I am sure there is no body of professional games players who so cheerfully know so little of the rules of their game as do professional golfers."

Henry Longhurst, 1959

"When I first learned of a mulligan in American golf I was astonished."

Tommy Armour, 1959

"I am always, I am afraid, liable to bore on the subject of the Rules of Golf but really it does seem to be ridiculous to have 93, and after the last lot of changes, possibly 100 pages of Rules of hitting a little ball about with a stick."

Henry Longhurst, 1967

"Forty-one rules aren't so many—St. Benedict had 73 to keep the brethren on the straight and narrow."

Colman McCarthy, 1977

"The rules should be written on the back of an envelope."

Henry Longhurst

"While golf's rules may not be easily understood, they are based on sound principles of reasoning and logic."

Janet Seagle, 1989, curator
and librarian for the USGA

"Tee it up, keep hitting it until you hole out, and if you want to touch the ball for any reason, pick it up, drop it within one club's length, and count one penalty stroke."

Peter Thomson

"One of the first and most important results of the substitution of St. Andrews for Leith as the recognized capital of golf was the adoption of 18 holes as the recognized round."

Robert Browning, 1955

"Cheating and breaking the rules are two different things."

Seve Ballesteros, 1991

"The penalty incurred when a ball is lost or out-of-bounds is without question the most unfair, illogical and harsh penalty ever conceived by the U.S. Golf Association and Royal and Ancient Golf Club of St. Andrews."

Cary Middlecoff, 1987

"Golfers should not fail to realize that it is a game of great traditions, of high ideals of sportsmanship, one in which a strict adherence to the rules is essential."

Francis Ouimet, 1940

"The Rules of Golf are debated and discussed everywhere the game is played—and often are the subject of conversation when the weather prevents the game from being played."

Janet Seagle, 1989

"It is difficult to understand how it is possible to become a devotee of golf without at least becoming inquisitive about the code which governs its play."

Richard S. Tufts, 1960

"While the rule book provides for the unplayable lie, it says nothing about the unplayable shot."

Tony Lema, 1966

"It is indeed true that the ethics of play in golf are very high and that those who fail to conform to this standard simply do not receive invitations for friendly games or to compete in invitation events."

Richard S. Tufts, 1960

"You play the game by the rules and that in itself is an infallible mark of a gentleman of quality."

Tommy Armour

9

The Basics

Vince Lombardi was a proponent of teaching his players to block and tackle. He was actually a predictable coach. Lombardi's players simply executed the basics better than others. The same is true with golf. Those who master the basics—grip, stance and swing—have the best chance of attaining a higher degree of proficiency. Of course, there is that great intangible of heart, or competitive spirit that separates the winners from the losers.

It begins with the grip, and while there are some minor differences, the grips of the better players are very similar. That doesn't mean the overlapping grip has to be the one employed. Gene Sarazen and Jack Nicklaus both used an interlocking grip and each won more than their share of championships and tournaments.

The stance is important to give the golfer the proper foundation and correct alignment. Some are wider than others and will vary because of the size of the golfer. Still there is a sameness to the stance which is evident when you watch professional golfers on a practice tee.

Some have observed that many of the professionals have a different swing, however. They may not look alike, but at the "moment of truth," that time when the club is swinging through the ball, they are very much the same.

Most golfers would be well advised to see a professional to work on the basics. Even tournament players who find themselves in a slump discover a breakdown of grip, stance or swing. The discovery and correction usually comes from another professional.

As wonderful a golfer as Bobby Jones was, he would occasionaly find there was a problem which he couldn't solve by himself. One time, he was not playing well on the eve of a tournament and he called Stewart Maiden, the professional who was Jones's only teacher. Maiden took a train and arrived the next day. He observed Jones hit about three shots on the practice tee and said, "Why don't you hit the ball with your backswing? It's fast enough." With that he left on the next train to Atlanta. It was all that had to be said. Jones realized he was swinging too fast, slowed his tempo and won the championship.

Ask most teaching professionals and the answer is usually the same. The problem lies in the grip, stance or swing. Equipment may change. Courses change. The basics remain.

————————

THE GRIP

"Without a proper grip, no golfer can expect to hit accurate shots with even a fair degree of consistency."

Gary Player, 1967

"With a good grip, a little ability and a lot of desire, anybody can become a good golfer."

Deacon Palmer

"A baseball bat is held with the hands. So are oars. But you hold a golf club with your fingers."

Tony Lema, 1966

"Take hold of a golf club with the same firmness that you shake hands with a friend."

Johnny Farrell, 1952

"The overlapping variety is often associated with the name of Harry Vardon. He did not invent it, but he is the man who was largely responsible for making it the accepted grip for nearly all competent golfers."

Henry Longhurst, 1937

"Don't ever worry about the grip not being tight enough."

Sam Snead, 1954

THE STANCE

"It is impossible to be fully relaxed and set up in a comfortable position for both the backswing and the downswing if your weight is on your toes."

Sam Snead, 1954

"It is a common fault to get into the position of the stance and then look at the line of flight."

Johnny Farrell, 1952

"A good way to take your stance is to perform a deep knee bend. The foot position which gives you the most secure balance is your correct stance for hitting a golf ball."

Tony Lema, 1966

"The stance should be wide enough to provide balance, but not so wide as to restrict freedom of movement."

Gary Player, 1967

"On every shot—driver or nine-iron—complete balance is what you strive for, and it is the proper stance which provides it."

Johnny Farrell, 1952

"In taking a proper stance, you should place your feet about as far apart as the width of your shoulders, that is for all full shots."

Byron Nelson, 1946

The Swing

"Golf is an awkward set of bodily contortions designed to produce a graceful result."

Tommy Armour

"The heart of the golf swing is the knee action."

Tony Lema, 1966

"There is no greater feeling in the world than to know you can't hook a golf ball."

Tommy Bolt

"What would seem to be the simple act of hitting a golf ball is actually one of the clumsiest movements imaginable, as any golfer who has ever tried to think about it while doing it will testify."

Charles Price, 1962

"An excellent way to practice your swing is to stand with your back to the sun and watch your shadow to see how much your head moves—or doesn't."

Don Herold, 1952

"Eighty percent of all golfers never finish the backswing before the downswing is under way."

Grantland Rice

"You control the swing with the left hand, you hit the ball with the right—in that order."

Brian Swarbrick, 1972

"On the backswing you are not lifting, pushing, or pulling the club— you are swinging it."

Johnny Farrell, 1952

"There is a slight variation in the swing from club to club, but, you should not make a conscious effort to swing one club differently than another."

Byron Nelson, 1946

"The idea in developing a golf swing is to do as many things correctly as you can, progressively. One good move leads to the next. And one bad move can ruin the whole thing."

Gary Player, 1967

"Golf is a game that is measured in yards, but the difference between a hit and a miss is calipered in micro-millimeters."

Tony Lema, 1966

"When you realize that a golf club positions the player's hands 40 inches, more or less, from a ball 1.68 inches in diameter that must be hit precisely after a swing that may take the clubhead on a round trip of as much as 26 or 27 feet, you become aware of the importance of using clubs conforming correctly to your requirements."

Tommy Armour, 1959

"The simpler you make your swing, the more you let your body go with your hands, the better the swing."

Sam Snead, 1954

"A golf swing seems simple only to the novice who doesn't know the first thing about it."

Stephen Baker, 1962

"You're not going to find a golf swing in a book."

Tony Lema, 1966

"Golf is a game of misses. With all the variables involved in striking a golf ball, it is impossible for anyone to achieve a flawless swing, perfect impact, and ideal flight, shot after shot."

Bob Toski

10

Putting

It is hard for me to remember any year passing by without some golfing friend showing off a new putter that was to eliminate all of his problems on the greens forever. They come in various shapes and sizes. Once fashioned strictly of wood or metal, now they are made out of plastic, lucite, crystal and space-age materials. There is no question in my mind that more time has been devoted to designing putters than the rest of the clubs combined. That's understandable, because putting is a mystery.

Golfers tend to blame their putters rather than themselves when they do not perform well on the green. While it is legend and not fact, an entertaining story is told of Ky Laffoon, a colorful professional of the '30s and '40s. Known as "The Chief" because of his resemblance to an American Indian, Ky's temper was legendary. The story is that Laffoon would tie his putter to the bumper of his car as he drove from one tournament to the next to punish it for too many three-putts. After dragging it for a considerable distance, he would bring it in the car and talk to it. He would say to the putter, "If you promise not to three-putt next week, I'll let you ride in the car all the way next time." I spoke with Ky about the story and he told me it wasn't true, but he never denied the story when it was told since he enjoyed the notoriety.

If par figures are attained by hitting every green in regulation, then putting is half of the game. Since it is rare to reach all of the greens in regulation, then the percentage is less, but that doesn't diminish the importance of putting. Even the greatest of putters will have off days and some never master the skill.

For some reason, the great putters are much maligned, as if it is not part of golf. They seem to be second-class citizens when compared with the shotmakers. When Billy Casper won the 1959 U.S. Open at Winged Foot, all of the reports were of his superb putting. It was as if he couldn't hit the ball, just putt. Considering that he shot 282 to win the championship, he must have done more than hit ground balls from tee to green. Golf historians recount the putting of Bobby Locke, but not his other shots, yet his four British Open titles must have included decent shotmaking as well.

Ben Hogan has said that golf is really two games, one played in the air and the other on the ground. Gene Sarazen was very serious when he proposed to have the hole enlarged. "Wild Bill" Mehlhorn asserted he was the worst putter who ever lived.

In the grill after the round, more stories are told about missed putts than about drives hit into the rough or out-of-bounds.

———

"Putting is a fascinating, aggravating, wonderful, terrible and almost incomprehensible part of the game of golf."

Arnold Palmer

"Long putts travel on the wings of chance."

Bernard Darwin

"When all is said and done, and whatever the method and whoever the man, successful putting surely must be a matter more of nerve than technique."

Pat Ward-Thomas, 1936

"I doubt if anyone ever hits two putts in succession exactly alike."

Walter Hagen, 1929

"A ball which is played with exactly the right strength will sometimes drop in from the side of the hole; a ball that is played a yard too hard never will."

John L. Low, 1903

"The good putter is not the man who runs up stone-dead every time, but he who holes out confidently at from five to six feet."

W. L. Watson

"Putting is a form of self-torture by which I have been fascinated throughout my golfing life."

Henry Longhurst, 1954

"Play the ball off the toe of the left foot. On Tuesdays, Thursdays and Saturdays play it off the right foot, which tends to place you nearer the hole and makes the putt look shorter."

Robinson Murray, 1951

"It does not matter whether you are Open Champion or a player with no handicap—you start level once your ball gets on the putting surface."

Henry Cotton, 1952

"When a putter is waiting his turn to hole out a putt of one or two feet in length, on which the match hangs on the last hole, it is of vital importance to think of nothing."

Sir Walter Simpson, 1887

"If the surface gleams, I know the green is fast and if it's dull, slow."

Cary Middlecoff

"One of the most destructive faults in putting is looking up, or moving the head."

Miller Barber

"I miss the hole. I miss the hole. I miss the hole. I hole it."

Seve Ballesteros, answering a
question on how he four-
putted the 16th at the 1988
Masters

"I believe the first rule for good putting is to take time enough to get settled, compose yourself, make peace with your God and the world, let the universe stop whirling, get the line right, get your grip right, rehearse, relax and shoot right. Don't putt muddled."

Don Herold, 1952

"The man who taught the world to putt was Walter Hagen."

Robert Browning

"The man who can putt is a match for anyone."

Willie Park, Jr.

"Putting is the department of golf which, more than any other, lends itself to experimentation and the exploitation of pet theories."

Harry Vardon, 1922

"Sure, I can putt, but you can't putt the ball off the tee."

Billy Casper, 1966

"Every golfer should realize that when he misses a two-foot putt, he offsets his 250-yard drive in one single stroke."

Mark Harris

"I hit short putts and stroke the long ones."

Mildred "Babe" Zaharias

"Golf is two separate games. One game is played in the air, the other on the ground. If I had my way, I would make every green a funnel. You hit it and the ball spins into the hole."

Ben Hogan

"It isn't any big deal. It's no different than a guy changing putters."

Tom Kite, on his switch to
cross-handed style putting,
1989

"Certain individuals possess natural qualifications that enable them to succeed admirably in putting at the hole; but others, who often show great gifts for most of the other strokes, yet execute these particular shots desperately badly."

Arnaud Massy, 1911

"I know of no detail of the game in which practice is of greater value."

Harry Vardon, 1922

"Many golfers enjoy putting to such an extent that they take three or four putts to the green."

Grantland Rice, 1926

"The greatest I ever saw at short putts was Johnny Revolta."

Tommy Armour

"The really good putter is largely born, not made, and is inherently endowed with a good eye and a tactile delicacy of grip which are denied the ordinary run of mortals."

Walter Travis

"A good putter can be made."

Claude Harmon

"Putting may be a matter of inspiration, but at least it has its material aspects."

Henry Longhurst, 1937

"You will never really deserve the name of golfer till you putt out your ball in two strokes, or even sometimes in one."

Arnaud Massy, 1911

"The game would be nothing without this troublesome business round the hole."

Joyce Wethered

"Those longish second putts take a lot out of you even when you make 'em."

Cary Middlecoff

"Putting can be a joy or the worst kind of frustration."

                                              Billy Casper

"It is generally true that the more proficient a golfer becomes, the greater will be his awareness of putting."

                                   Pat Ward-Thomas, 1966

"My first objective in putting has always been to impart topspin to the ball."

                                            Bobby Locke

"Advice is the commonest and cheapest commodity on the golf course. One place to completely ignore it is on the greens."

                                       Jack Nicklaus

"Holing pressure putts isn't a matter of inherited talent or divine inspiration."

                                       George Archer

"Accept the fact that you have no control over the ball once it leaves the putter."

                                       Bruce Crampton

"Putting can drive you a bit crackers."

                                       Sandy Lyle

"The putting stroke should be as simple as possible."

                                       Billy Casper

"Once you've had 'em, you've got 'em."

Tommy Armour, on the yips

"When people say the greens are too fast, let them look to their own putting and see if the fault does not lie there."

Bernard Darwin, 1936

"There are two T's in putting—Technique and Thought."

Jerome Travers, 1933

"On putts of six feet or less, concentrate on starting the ball on a line that you like for the first three inches. Sight an imaginary three-inch line and get the putt started right."

Vic Ghezzi

"Probably the most important fundamental in putting is to avoid moving the body during the stroke, or at least until the ball has been hit."

Jim Barnes, 1925

"Good putting is half confidence. The only way to secure confidence is by practice."

Jerome Travers, 1913

"The secret of successful putting is to have a clear mental picture of the path that the ball has to take, and to shut out all confusing thoughts of the ways in which it may conceivably be missed."

Charles Whitcombe, 1949

"Putting calls for the highest degree of skill and the nicest kind of judgment both as regards accuracy and strength."

Walter Travis, 1901

"You can cover 400 yards with two strokes, hole after hole, day after day. And then you take three or four more to cover the last 20 feet. Does this make any sense?"

Lee Trevino, 1989

"When I start putting bad, I tend to look for miracles. I tell myself, 'It can't be my stroke,' but it usually is."

Arnold Palmer, 1988

"The best players are not always the best putters, but bad putters almost never become champions."

Bob Rosburg

"Why didn't I win more? I was the world's worst puter."

"Wild Bill" Mehlhorn

"You can tell a good putt by the sound it makes."

Bobby Locke

"If you gave me only one word to describe putting, I would say, 'feel'."

Billy Casper

"The nerves are the first thing to go in putting."

Sam Snead

"I have to admit I'm probably the best putter in the world."

George Low

"No man has yet been able to win a championship without putting well."

Robert T. Jones, Jr.

"Very early in my career I realized that putting was half the game of golf."

Bobby Locke

"I don't think the girls are better putters. I think the men have the edge."

Nancy Lopez

"First off, there's no right or wrong way to putt."

Fuzzy Zoeller

"Putts longer than a foot should not be conceded."

Horton Smith

"The greatest five, in my book, are Walter J. Travis, Jerry Travers, Bob Jones, Walter Hagen and Horton Smith."

Grantland Rice

"There is only one mechanical secret to putting, in my confirmed opinion, and this is holding still."

Arnold Palmer

"My personal opinion is that more men are good putters from practice than because they have any pronounced superiority, to begin with, over other men."

Francis Ouimet

"When you are lining up a long putt, choose a spot part way to the cup that you want the ball to run over."

Johnny Farrell, 1952

"Putting, in fact, is a game in itself."

Bobby Locke

"You can always recover from a bad drive, but there's no recovering from a bad putt. It's missing those six-inchers that causes guys to break their sticks."

Jimmy Demaret

"Much of the bewilderment about putting is caused by failure to apply some elementary reasoning."

Joe Novak

"One could no more undertake to produce a perfect putt at every attempt, than one could undertake the perfect poem."

Arnold Haultain

"Bill, that was the dumbest putt I ever saw."

Lloyd Mangrum, to
Bill Hyndman after he putted
off the green and into the
water on the 11th hole at the
Masters, 1959

"I guess I putt past the pin more than most anyone."

Arnold Palmer

"The disease is universal, and there is no known antidote."

Peter Alliss, about the yips,
1981

"It is amazing how much even a short putt will veer off line because of a slight head movement."

Arnold Palmer

"The less said about the putter the better. Here is an instrument of torture, designed by Tantalus and forged in the devil's own smithy."

Tony Lema, 1966

"Putting is an inexact science. There are many good putters who use vastly different techniques to accomplish the same results."

Gary Player, 1967

11

Advice

Possibly the single most important event to serve as the spring-board for the popularity of golf in America was the 1913 U.S. Open. The two biggest names in golf, Harry Vardon and Ted Ray, were in the country for a series of exhibitions. They also played in some tournaments, one of which was the U.S. Open. There was little doubt that they would be favorites when the championship began at The Country Club. At the end of 72 holes they were tied and an 18-hole playoff was set to determine the champion. The surprise was that they were joined by a third golfer, young Francis Ouimet, an ex-caddie at the host club.

While there was hope among the Americans, the favorites had to be the two Britishers. Ouimet's caddie throughout the championship was 10-year-old Eddie Lowery. On the day of the playoff, Ouimet's friend, Frank Hoyt, asked if he could caddie for him and Francis told Hoyt to talk it over with Eddie. An offer of some money was made to Lowery, but he would not accept and his eyes began to well up with tears. There would be no change in caddies.

Here was Ouimet about to play for the most important golf title in the United States, against the two best-known golfers in the world. To say he was a bit excited and nervous would be a gross under-statement. Little Eddie Lowery handed Ouimet his driver and said, "Be sure and keep your eye on the ball." That a caddie would give such advice to a man about to play his most important round was laughable, but it had the proper effect and Ouimet went on to win the title. The statement became part of golfing lore.

That same advice has been given or received by almost every golfer, although it comes in different forms such as "Keep your head down" or

"Don't move your head" or "Watch the ball." I have been at golf resorts, wanting to play and asked to be put with others since I didn't have a game. More than once I have begun the round with five or six pars only to hit the next drive into the woods or the rough. Immediately, one of the golfers who hasn't scored better than a double-bogey on any hole and thinks that moving the ball through the green is a part of the game, will tell me what I did wrong. I know what I did wrong—I hit a lousy shot and before the round is over, I'll hit some others.

I'm not sure how many golf instruction books have been written, but there are at least 700 in my golf library. In fact, nearly half my golf library consists of instruction books. Long ago I gave up reading them but I usually skim the books to see if there is any mention made of a specific tournament or golfer. There are exceptions, such as when I acquire a very old book with an interesting writing style. I've found there is little difference in the 700 chapters on the proper grip, for example.

Good or ill, invited or not, advice has always been a part of golf and likely it will continue to be that way.

———

"It's a fun game. So, have fun."

Tony Lema, 1966

"The main difficulty, and the obstacle which trips most hopefuls before they step up on the first tee, is that they try to remember too many separate bits of instruction."

Oscar Fraley, 1952

"The ball must be straight before your breast, a little towards the left foot."

Thomas Kincaid, 1687

"Timing the stroke properly is of vast importance. Usually the player is in too much of a hurry to get the shot away, and hits too soon."

Walter Travis, 1901

"If your adversary is badly bunkered, there is no rule against your standing over him and counting his strokes aloud, with increasing gusto as their number mounts up; but it will be a wise precaution to arm yourself with the niblick before doing so, so as to meet him on equal terms."

Horace Hutchinson, 1886

"Stand firm and don't sway or look up."

Harold Hilton, 1903

"Betake yourself of a tutor of some kind and set yourself on the right path at the beginning of your journey."

Henry Longhurst, 1937

"Instead of trying to maneuver the ball with your body, arms and hands, trust your swing and the club you select for the shot."

Ben Hogan

"The winding-up of the trunk is essential in good golf."

Henry Cotton, 1948

"It is absolutely necessary to plan your round before you tee off."

Peter Thomson, 1961

"The apprentice golfer should, in the first instance, burden himself only with the strict minimum of clubs. He will do well to confine himself to the driver, the brassy, the iron, the mashie and the putter."
Arnaud Massy, 1911

"Force yourself to pause between shots. Never rush through practice."
Gary Player, 1966

"The speed of one's swing is of little importance so long as it is smooth and unified."
Byron Nelson, 1966

"If your head doesn't move your body doesn't sway and you maintain a stable axis for your swing."
Tommy Armour, 1959

"Six clubs are all a beginner needs, driver, brassie, cleek, mid-iron, mashie and putter. After he learns how to use these he can add a mashie niblick for the task of getting out of bunkers and sand traps, and a jigger for running up short approaches,"
Jerome Travers, 1913

"Approach each shot carefully but casually. Hit and run golf never got anybody to first base. Hurry has no part in the sport. It is a game of leisure."
Walter Hagen

"I never think of anything at the address except hitting the ball."
Robert T. Jones, Jr.

"Watch out for busses."

> **Ben Hogan,** responding to a
> question if he had any advice
> to today's young players, 1990

"One should hit the ball in a carefree way, but not carelessly."

> **Chick Evans**

"Shorten your back swing and take the club back with your wrists. Swing easily, and keep your eye on the ball."

> **Alex Smith**

"All the pros can teach you to hit the 'intentional slice.' It's the unintentional slice we have to work on."

> **Jim Murray**

"Don't be deluded by driving range yardage markers."

> **Brian Swarbrick,** 1972

"The next one."

> **Walter Hagen,** responding to
> a question about which is the
> most important shot in golf

"Get started right. That is doubtless the most important bit of advice an expert can give the man who is ambitious to learn to play golf and play it well."

> **Jerome Travers,** 1913

"Golf is a two-handed affair. The clubhead and the hands, wrists and arms should be considered as parts of the club, all working together as one piece of machinery."

Harry Vardon

"If you can't break 80, you have no business on the golf course. If you can, you have no business."

Jack Berry, in
The Detroit News, 1991

"If you hit a ball with a mashie it will sometimes go farther than if you miss it with a driver."

Ring Lardner

"No golfer ever gets so consistently good that he can't use some constructive advice. No matter how many trophies he may win, he can't analyze and remedy his own faults."

Byron Nelson, 1946

"Practice should be approached as just about the most pleasant recreation ever devised, besides being a necessary part of golf."

Mildred "Babe" Zaharias

"Don't take the club back too quickly. This advice can surely never change."

Henry Cotton, 1952

"Use the club that gives you the best chance of getting the job done, no matter what you see others using."

Brian Swarbrick, 1973

"I am convinced that exercises with Indian clubs and dumbbells are not for the good of the golfer, because they disturb the condition of the golfing muscles."

Henry Cotton, 1952

"My wife told me to quit giving lessons and start taking them."

Phil Rodgers

"One thing that will help you keep calm while playing golf is to remember that nobody gives a darn about your bad golf but you."

Don Herold, 1952

"The tyro then ought to be fully convinced of the difficulty of the game and the paramount necessity of studying it seriously, if he wished ever to succeed."

Arnaud Massy, 1911

"You can talk to a fade, but a hook won't listen."

Lee Trevino

"There is almost irresistible temptation to let your mind wander in golf. But you've got to concentrate, concentrate, concentrate!"

Tommy Armour, 1959

"Your objective in golf is to groove your swing—to make it so natural that you could hit a ball blindfolded."

Johnny Farrell, 1950

"The keynote of the address position should be ease, comfort and relaxation."

Robert T. Jones, Jr., 1955

"On any golf shot, once you have addressed the ball properly, the most important single act you can perform is to pause between your backswing and your downswing."

Jack Burke, Jr., 1952

"Tee the ball low, rejecting the very prevalent but erroneous idea that you are more certain of getting it away cleanly and well when it is teed high off the ground."

Harry Vardon, 1905

"You can transmit your power to the club-head through only one medium—the hands with which you hold the club, not the legs, the shoulders or other parts."

Ernest Jones, 1953

"Beware the common mistake of confusing concentration on the ball and becoming hypnotized by it."

Johnny Farrell, 1950

"I would recommend all golfers to model their styles upon the recognized lines that have stood the test of decades of play at the hands of the best amateurs and professionals."

Willie Park, 1896

"It does you no good to practice after a round when you are feeling tired, or at any time when your coordination is worn down."

Gene Sarazen, 1950

"You can't control when you win, all you can control is how you play and your emotions and yourself."

Peter Kosti

"I've never had a coach. If I find one who can beat me, then I'll listen."

Lee Trevino, 1991

"Practicing from the rough teaches you how to swing through the ball, which you must do or you just aren't going to get much distance."

Gary Player, 1967

"Never listen to a golf tip; never practice; never get old and fat at the same time."

Dave Kindred, 1991

"If I were starting golf all over, I'd take lessons for a year before playing a round."

Don Herold, 1952

"Slow down under pressure."

Tom Watson, 1991

"I am firmly convinced there is no such thing as a straight left arm at the position where so many golfers have been informed there is. A straight left arm at the top of the backward swing is impossible in anything approaching a correct movement."

Harry Vardon

"Without the straight left arm it is well-nigh impossible to ever become a consistently good golfer, for there is too much leeway for error."

Gene Sarazen

"In the last analysis, you make all your own breaks—in golf as in life."

Arnold Palmer, 1963

"Some of the best ideas I've had on golf have been some I've thought up myself while the pro was talking about something else."

Don Herold, 1952

"You can improve your game 100 percent by quitting."

Jack Berry, in
The Detroit News, 1991

BIBLIOGRAPHY

A Golf Story by Charles Price. New York; Antheneum, 1986.

A Guide to Good Golf by James Barnes. New York; Dodd, Mead, 1925.

A History of Golf in Great Britain by Bernard Darwin. London; Cassell, 1952.

A Round of Golf with Tommy Armour by Tommy Armour. New York; Simon & Schuster, 1959.

All About Putting by the Editors of *Golf Digest*. New York; Coward, McCann & Geoghegan, 1973.

The American Golfer edited by Charles Price. New York; Random House, 1964.

Are Golfers Human? by Robinson Murray. New York; Prentice-Hall, 1951.

Arnold Palmer by the Editors of *Golf Digest*. New York; Grosset & Dunlop, 1967.

At Random Through the Green compiled by John Stobbs. New York; Meredith Press, 1966.

The Best of Golf by Peter Alliss and Bob Ferrier. London; Partridge Press, 1989.

The Best of Henry Longhurst by Henry Longhurst. Norwalk, CT; *Golf Digest,* 1987.

The Bobby Jones Story by Grantland Rice from the writings of O.B. Keeler. Atlanta; Tupper & Love, 1953.

Buick Open tournament program edited by John A. Hewig. Sports Marketing International, 1989.

Champagne Tony's Golf Tips by Tony Lema. New York, McGraw-Hill, 1966.

The Complete Golfer by Harry Vardon. London; Methuen, 1905.

The Complete Golfer edited by Herbert Warren Wind. New York; Simon and Schuster, 1954.

Confessions of a Hooker by Bob Hope. Garden City, NY; Doubleday & Company, 1985.

Concerning Golf by John L. Low. London; Hodder & Stoughton, 1903

Down the Nineteenth Fairway edited by Peter Dobereiner. London, William Collins Sons, 1982.

The Duffer's Guide to Bogey Golf by Brian Swarbrick. New York, Prentice-Hall, 1973.

The Duffer's Handbook of Golf by Grantland Rice and Clare Briggs. New York; MacMillan & Co., 1926. Reprinted in 1988 by The Classics of Golf.

Education of a Golfer by Sam Snead. New York; Simon & Schuster, 1962.

85th U. S. Open edited by Bev Norwood. Far Hills, NJ; U.S.G.A., 1985.

86th U. S. Open edited by Bev Norwood. Far Hills, NJ; U.S.G.A., 1986.

87th U. S. Open edited by Bev Norwood. Far Hills, NJ; U.S.G.A., 1987.

Esquire's World of Golf by Herb Graffis. New York; Simon and Schuster, 1965.

The Essential Henry Longhurst by Henry Longhurst. London; Willow Books, 1988.

The Fifty Greatest Golfers by Peter Dobereiner. New York; Gallery Books, 1957.

Fifty Years of American Golf by H. B. Martin. New York; Dodd, Mead, 1936.

Fifty Years of Golf by Horace G. Hutchinson. London; Country Life, 1919.

Fifty Years of Golf: My Memories by Andra Kirkaldy. London; Unwin Bros., 1921.

Following Through by Herbert Warren Wind. New York; Ticknor & Fields, 1985.

The Game with the Hole in it by Peter Dobereiner. London, Faber and Faber, 1970.

Gettin' to the Dance Floor by Al Barkow. New York; Antheneum, 1986.

The Gist of Golf by Harry Vardon. New York; George H. Doran, 1922.

Golf by Charles Whitcombe. London; Sir Isaac Pitman & Sons, 1949.

Golf by Arnaud Massy. London; Methuen & Co. Ltd., 1914.

Golf: A Royal and Ancient Game by Robert Clark. Edinburgh; printed for R. & R. Clark, 1875.

Golf Digest - Trumbull, CT

Golf Magazine - New York

Golf Between Two Wars by Bernard Darwin. London; Chatto Windus, 1944.

The Golf Book edited by Michael Bartlett. New York; Arbor House, 1980.

Golf from a New Angle by Theodore Moone. London; Trinity Press, 1934.

The Golf Immortals by Tom Scott and Geoffrey Cousins. New York; Hart Publishing Company, 1969.

Golf in Action by Oscar Fraley. New York; A. A. Wyn, 1952.

Golf Is My Business by Norman von Nida. London; Frederick Muller Ltd., 1956.

Golf: Its History, People and Events by Will Grimsley. Englewood Cliffs; Prentice-Hall, 1966.

Golf: The Golden Years compiled by Sarah Baddiel. London; Bestseller Publications, 1989.

Golf: The Great Ones by Michael McDonnell. New York; Drake Publishers, Inc., 1973.

Golf World' Magazine - Southern Pines, NC

The Golfer's Companion edited by Peter Lawless. London; J. M. Dent, 1937.

Golfer's Digest 5th Edition edited by Earl Puckett. Chicago, Follett Publishing, 1972.

Golfer's Digest 6th Edition edited by Earl Puckett. Northfield, IL, Digest Books, 1974.

Golfer's Digest 7th Edition edited by Earl Puckett and Robert Cromie. Chicago, Follett Publishing, 1975.

Golfers' Gold by Tony Lema. New York; Little, Brown & Co., 1964.

The Golfer's Manual by A Keen Hand (Henry Brougham Farnie). St. Andrews, Cupar; Whitehead and Orr, 1857.

The Golfers Own Book edited by Dave Stanley and George G. Ross. New York, Latern Press, 1956.

The Golfer's Year Book edited by William D. Richardson and Lincoln A. Werden. New York; The Golfer's Year Book Co., Inc., 1931.

Golfing By-Paths by Bernard Darwin. London; Country Life, 1948.

Golf's Golden Grind by Al Barkow. New York; Harcourt Brace, Jovanovich, 1974.

Golf's Magnificent Challenge by Robert Trent Jones. Sammis Publishing, 1988.

Great Golf Courses of the World by William H. Davis and the editors of *Golf Digest*. Norwalk, CT; *Golf Digest,* 1974.

Great Golfers in the Making by H. B. Martin. New York; Dodd, Mead & Company, 1932.

Herbert Warren Wind's Golf Book by Herbert Warren Wind. New York; Simon and Schuster, 1971.

Hints on Golf by Horace Hutchinson. London; William Blackwood and Sons, 1886.

The Hole Truth by Tommy Bolt. Philadelphia; J. B. Lippincott Co., 1971.

How to Play Golf in the Low 120's by Stephen Baker. Englewood Cliffs, NJ; Prentice-Hall, 1962.

100 Greatest Golf Courses - and then some by William H. Davis and the editors of *Golf Digest*. Norwalk, CT; *Golf Digest,* 1982.

James Braid by Bernard Darwin. London; Hodder & Stoughton, 1952.

Ladies in the Rough by Glenna Collett. New York; Alfred P. Knopf, 1928.

The Lay of the Land edited by Herbert Warren Wind and Robert Macdonald from the golf writings of Pat Ward-Thomas. Stamford, The Classics of Golf, 1990.

The Long Green Fairway by Pat Ward-Thomas. London; Hodder & Stoughton, Ltd., 1966.

Love that Golf by Don Herold. New York; A. S. Barnes, 1952.

The Masters by Dick Schaap. New York; Random House, 1970.

Mostly Golf edited by Peter Ryde. London; Adam and Charles Black, 1977.

My Game and Yours by Arnold Palmer. New York; Simon and Schuster, 1963.

My Partner, Ben Hogan by Jimmy Demaret. New York; McGraw-Hill, 1954.

The Mystery of Golf by Arnold Haultain. London; Constable, 1908.

Only on Sundays by Henry Longhurst. London; Caswell, 1964.

The Open Championship 1984 edited by Bev Norwood. Windlesham, England; Springwood Books, 1984.

Par Golf in 8 Steps by Joe Novak. New York; Prentice-Hall, 1951.

Peter Alliss An Autobiography by Peter Alliss. London; William Collins Sons, 1981.

The Pictorial History of Golf by Ian Morrison. New York; Gallery Books, 1990.

Playing Through by William Wartman. New York; William Morrow and Company, Inc., 1990.

Positive Golf by Gary Player. New York; McGraw Hill, 1967

Practical Golf by Walter Travis. New York; Harper & Brothers, 1901.

The Principles Behind the Rules of Golf by Richard S. Tufts, Pinehurst, NC, by the author, 1960.

PRO: Frank Beard on the Golf Tour by Dick Schaap. New York; World Publishing Company, 1974.

Reminiscences of Golf on St. Andrews Links by James Balfour. Edinbrough; David Douglas, 1897.

The Rules of Golf by Francis Ouimet. Garden City, NY; Garden City Publishing, 1948.

St. Andrews, Home of Golf by James K. Robertson. Cupar, Fife, Scotland; J. & G. Innis, 1967.

St. Andrews, Home of Golf by Louis T. Stanley. Topsfield, MA; Salem House, 1986.

Sam Snead's Natural Golf edited by Tom Shehan. New York, A. S. Barnes and Company, 1953.

The Scottish Invasion by Richard S. Tufts. Pinehurst, NC; Pinehurst Publishers, 1962.

Scotland's Gift: Golf; Reminiscences 1872–1927 by Charles Blair Macdonald. New York; Charles Scribner's Sons, 1928.

The Secrets of Perfect Putting by Horton Smith and Dawson Taylor. North Hollywood; Wilshire Book Co., 1978.

The Snake in the Sandtrap (and Other Misadventures on the Golf Tour) by Lee Trevino and Sam Blair. New York; Holt, Rinehart and Winston, 1985.

The Sporting World of Jim Murray by Jim Murray. Garden City, NY; Doubleday & Company, Inc., 1968.

The Sport of Princes by Laddie Lucas. London; Stanley Paul, 1978.

Sports Illustrated Magazine - Los Angeles.

The Squire by John M. Olman. Cincinnati; Olman Industries, Inc., 1987.

The Story of American Golf by Herbert Warren Wind. New York; Alfred A. Knopf, 1948.

The Story of the Open Golf Championship by Charles G. Mortimer. London; Jarrolds, 1952.

Superstars of Golf by Nick Seitz. Norwalk, CT, *Golf Digest*, 1978.

Thirty Years of Championship Golf by Gene Sarazen. New York; Prentice-Hall, Inc., 1950.

Travers' Golf Book by Jerome D. Travers. New York; The Macmillan Company, 1913.

A Tribute to Golf edited by Thomas P. Stewart. Harbor Springs, Michigan; Stewart, Hunter & Associates, 1990.

The Tumult and the Shouting by Grantland Rice. New York; A. S. Barnes & Company, 1954.

The Walter Hagen Story by Walter Hagen. New York; Simon and Schuster, 1956.

The Weekend Golfer by Johnny Farrell. London, Herbert Jenkins Ltd., 1952.

Winning Golf by Byron Nelson. New York, A. S. Barnes, 1946.

The World Atlas of Golf edited by Pat Ward-Thomas. London, Mitchell Beazley Publishing, 1976.

The World Atlas of Golf Courses by Bob Ferrier. New York, Mallard Press, 1990.

The World of Golf by Charles Price. New York; Random House, 1962.

The World of Golf edited by Gordon Menzies. London; British Broadcast Corporation, 1982.

Index to Illustrations by Doug Parrish

Index to quotations

Page numbers in bold type refer to quotations attributed to the individual; non-bold numbers refer to quotations about the individual or topic.